MW01199891

WELL-ORDERED FAMILY

WELL-ORDERED FAMILY

CONOR GALLAGHER

TAN Books
Gastonia, North Carolina

Well-Ordered Family © 2024 Conor Gallagher

All rights reserved. With the exception of short excerpts used in critical review, no part of this work may be reproduced, transmitted, or stored in any form whatsoever, without the prior written permission of the publisher. Creation, exploitation, and distribution of any unauthorized editions of this work, in any format in existence now or in the future—including but not limited to text, audio, and video—is prohibited without the prior written permission of the publisher.

Unless otherwise noted, Scripture quotations are from the Revised Standard Version of the Bible—Second Catholic Edition (Ignatius Edition), copyright © 2006 National Council of the Churches of Christ in the United States of America. Used by permission. All rights reserved.

Cover & interior design by David Ferris, www.davidferrisdesign.com

Library of Congress Control Number: 2024935646
ISBN: 978-1-5051-3415-5
Kindle ISBN: 978-1-5051-3418-6
ePUB ISBN: 978-1-5051-3417-9

Published in the United States by
TAN Books
PO Box 269
Gastonia, NC 28053

Printed in the United States of America

To Ashley, Aiden, Mary, Patrick, Peter, Jude, Paul, Teresa, Imelda, David, Annie, Luke, Thomas, Lucy, Lily Jane, Elizabeth, and any future children if God wills it so.

Thank you for teaching me everything in this book.

CONTENTS

THIS BOOK IS JUST
THE BEGINNING

Scan the QR code on this page to go to our website:

WellOrderedFamily.com

With the aim of best serving you and your family for the years to come, QR codes are displayed frequently throughout this book. These codes link directly to specific tools on our website. On the site, we give you more ideas and examples of how to use each tool, plus the opportunity to download your own blank version.

If you are holding the printed copy in your hands, please use it as a reference book. Highlight, fill in the blanks, and attach sticky notes where it's most helpful.

INTRODUCTION

You love your family. You want to bring more order and clarity to your family life. Families feel overwhelmed by the chaos of modern life. Chaos is not creativity. It's not freedom. Chaos makes everyone anxious, crazed, or even despondent. It is not good.

Contentment, creativity—and true freedom—depend on order. But to achieve order, you need a system.

There are three sure signs that your family doesn't have a family management system.

1. You feel too busy
2. Unnecessary conflict is a normal way of life
3. When it comes to family dynamics, you have little joy and loads of constant anxiety

Leave these conditions in place long enough and you get spouses who drift apart, teenagers who drift away, and a lingering grief that overwhelms you as you slowly realize you're failing those you love most.

It doesn't have to be this way.

Well-Ordered Family™ was founded to put an end to this.

My wife, Ashley, and I have fifteen children. Their names are Aiden, Mary, Patrick, Peter, Jude, Paul, Teresa, Imelda, David, Annie, Luke, Thomas, Lucy, Lily Jane, and Elizabeth. I love giving someone a name. In fact, many of my kids have multiple middle names, such as Luke Dominic Chesterton Gallagher, and his twin brother, Thomas Joshua Kolbe Gallagher. Giving someone a name is a tremendous honor. I take it very seriously. After all, I am a word nerd.

I'm terrible with numbers, however, so don't ask me their birthdates. I feel accomplished when I can work out the year. My wife Ashley, on the other hand, has the complete data for all fifteen at the tip of her tongue, including heights, weights, allergies, and Social Security numbers.

People often wonder about the makeup of our family. Can fifteen really be, well, *fifteen*? At the time this book goes to press, we have eight boys and seven girls. The oldest is twenty-two and the youngest is two. We have one set of twins (age six). And, in fact, we are expecting number sixteen, due shortly after the release of this book. It's a girl, which brings the total to eight and eight. Her name is Monica, named after Saint Augustine's mother, the patron saint of mothers. Ashley chose Monica as her patron before she had any kids. One must marvel at that providential choice. To date, we have been blessed with healthy children. It hasn't always been easy. My wife has experienced numerous miscarriages, and I plan on meeting these children at Heaven's Gate upon my arrival.

My wife and I know what a chaotic family life is all about. We know the joys and sorrows, the ups and downs. We know the dangers of technology, the trials and tribulations of friendships, of sports character-building that veers into sports fanaticism. We also know the chronic pressure of financial stress. We know how the same family can go from laughter to fighting in seconds. We've seen broken bones and broken hearts. We know what it's like to demand an apology from a child and what it feels like to apologize to a child. We know babies, toddlers, small children, middle schoolers, teenagers, and now, adult kids. We even have two grandchildren on the way, one of which will be older than her own Aunt Monica. No parent can experience everything, but we have experienced a lot.

We know how blessed we are to have these children. We are so proud of our children. But we also scratch our heads and wonder why we haven't done a better job in certain ways, or why we let the stress get to us at different times. We are happy. We are also remorseful. Why didn't we do better? Every child came along and reminded us that there is always room for improvement. We hope to be better tomorrow than we are today.

In addition to being the father of fifteen, I am also the CEO of multiple businesses. This wasn't always the case. As the first five or six kids arrived, a level of complexity entered our lives that we'd never known before. At that time, I was a young lawyer with a master's degree in philosophy. My first book was titled *If Aristotle's Kid Had an iPod: Ancient Wisdom for Modern Parents*. Its theme is what Aristotle can teach us about raising kids in the digital age. I mention this because I've always had a drive to get to the essence of an issue and to connect seemingly unconnected dots. For a mind of my particular bent, joining ancient Greek philosophy with modern attitudes toward smart phones and social media seemed natural.

I did not become a professional philosopher or remain a lawyer for very long.

Despite never taking a business class in my life, I eventually entered the business world. This is a story in itself, but suffice it to say I felt very unprepared for my new calling! In a frantic attempt to figure out what I was doing, I read approximately 250 business books (yes, I tried to count them one day). Read enough books on business methods and philosophy and you notice certain underlying principles recurring again and again. I pulled those principles together and developed what I call "the natural law of business." I use it constantly in my professional life.

So, there I was: a young businessman trying to bring order and clarity to business operations at work, and my wife was trying to bring order and clarity to our home. I noticed that our labors were not all that different (though hers was more important, more exhausting, and more rewarding). When I came home at night, I was excited about what I'd done during the day. Those principles of business were slowly but surely working!

I began to apply my business knowledge to the day-to-day running of the family. Doing so seemed a natural extension of my day. There were clear similarities and analogous situations. Why not give my natural laws of business a try?

I did, and they worked.

There was no bolt from the blue. It was the slow and steady accumulation of small successes that told the tale.

Today, I oversee multiple businesses. One way to think about a business is to picture a well-oiled machine. If you don't create order in your thoughts, actions, and communications, you will go out of business. The "check engine" light flashes on. Left unattended, the machine breaks. It's the same with a business. No order, no system or means to check it, means no commerce. The money stops flowing. One thing about us humans is that we pay *very* close attention when a sack of gold is on the line.

Now, fifteen children in, I am completely convinced that the principles of managing a well-ordered business apply to managing a well-ordered family. I'm not only going to prove it to you, I'm going to show you how to do it.

There are so many resources to help create a well-ordered business. But no one I'm aware of has taken the time to apply this knowledge to family life.

Here is the first "natural law of business": In its essence, business is the act of getting a group of people to work toward a shared vision.

Guess what a family is! It's a group of people working toward a shared vision, or at least it should be.

All too often, the executive at work focuses on getting his marketing department to communicate better with his finance department . . . and then goes home exhausted and does nothing to improve communication between his spouse and teenager. So often, people choose a job because of *company* culture but do little at home to make improvements to *family* culture. Seen from a distance, such a situation is not only messed up, it's nigh-on *immoral*. But here in the everyday fray, we are flawed, sinful human beings who—totally against our wishes, and contrary to everything we hold dear—perform better at work than we do at home. It feels crazy. It is *wrong*.

It is time for this to change.

We must be our very best with our families. Most of us feel called by God and conscience to be our best at home. But how? It may sound counterintuitive, but the business tools of corporate success can help us.

In The Well-Ordered Family Management System™, I provide a six-part process to reclaim order and clarity in your family life. I begin with vision for a few reasons. First, I believe there is great benefit to beginning with the end in mind. For this reason, vision becomes a foundation for the other five parts in the Family Management System™. Secondly, I have been asked what is lacking most in the modern American family in regards to my six-part system. My answer is vision. Families are spinning their wheels in part because they don't have a clear idea of where they want to go. And thus, I begin with vision.

It is important, however, for me to make something crystal clear: you do not have to work through these six parts in the sequence that I have set forth. I recognize that beginning with vision might be overly philosophical right now. If you want to focus right now on getting your family on the same page for this upcoming week, feel free to jump to part two on unity in which I discuss family meetings. If you feel the need to get control of screen time and cell phones immediately, consider part three on systems. If the idea of a family scorecard really piques your interest, you can begin with part four on metrics. Or perhaps you are suffering from deep conflict with a teenager or spouse. There are a few tools in part five on relationships that might give you some clarity in the next five minutes. What if you are on the verge of making a major decision such as buying a new car or taking a new job? Part six on discernment might be the perfect place for you to focus right now.

I have designed the Family Management System™ to be dynamic. Your family is different than mine. Your stressors are different than mine. Your family's strengths are different than my family's strengths. So, move at your own pace and your own sequence. And yet, I firmly believe that all six parts are steeped in the natural law that governs your family's well-being.

Most of us, however, have little time to master complex systems before seeing results. The demands of work and family come at us like water gushing from a fire hydrant. We need help! The philosophy can wait.

With this in mind, I've provided more than twenty-five tools to help you implement this family management system. A tool is a worksheet that makes the work a little easier. You might find only one or two of these tools effective for your family. No problem! My goal is to help you and your family get going in the right direction. Remember another of the natural laws of business: it's much better to do a few things well than to do many things poorly.

The goal is not order in itself, but a vibrant, meaningful family life. Businesses thrive on order, accountability, and vision. So can your family. I will show you how.

Here is a quick overview of the six parts of The Well-Ordered Family Management System™. You can use this overview to decide where you want to begin.

PART 1: VISION

Order and clarity begin with vision. Every business, every athletic team, and every significant achievement begins with having a crystal-clear vision of where you want to go. I will help you create your very own master plan using The Family Master Plan™.

Tools included:
- The Family Master Plan™
- The Family SWOT™
- The Family Vision+ Statement Builder™

Shape your vision.
- Craft your Family Vision+ Statement
- Perform a SWOT Analysis
- Discover your Core Virtues
- Choose a Family Patron, a Family Motto, and a Family Beatitude
- Envision a Ten-Year Family Portrait
- Target Three-Year Household Goals

PART 2: UNITY

It has been said that one percent of success is due to vision, but 99 percent of success comes with alignment around that vision. We call this unity. Nothing is more powerful in this world than a united family. In this part, we'll show you how to have family meetings to stay united around your vision.

Tools included:
* The Family Meeting Cadence Master List™
* Sample agendas for each family meeting

Learn to lead.
* The Weekly Marriage Check-In™
* The Weekly Family Huddle™
* The Quarterly Family Meeting™
* The Annual Family Council™

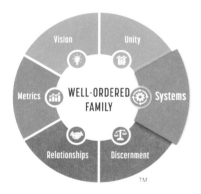

PART 3: SYSTEMS

This is the engine that drives family dynamics. Everything in life fits into a system, even if it is a really bad system. Families run on systems. In business, we break down systems into macrosystems (environments) and microsystems (processes). Families can do this, too.

Processes are those day-to-day routines that keep things running smoothly and bring a sense of peace into your home.

Tools included:
* The KFP Finalizer™
* The Digital Policy Builder™

Customize your essential family processes for order and clarity.

- Discover your KFPs (Key Family Processes)
- Use our numerous sample processes to customize your own Family Digital Policy

Environments include those large, external factors that shape your world.

Tool included:

- The Family STRREP Test™

Get a grip on the external forces acting on your family.

- Social factors
- Technological factors
- Religious factors
- Recreational factors
- Educational factors
- Professional factors

PART 4: METRICS

What gets measured gets managed. Great human achievements are usually accompanied with incredible attention to key data points that indicate success and failure. There are a handful of key metrics that your particular family should monitor on a weekly or monthly basis. We will help you discover these.

Tools included:

- The Family Scorecard Generator™
- The Family Habit Tracker™

People *respect* what you *inspect*. Learn how to simplify the way you track the most important numbers and activities in your family life.

- Rank the most important areas in your family life
- Craft measures of success so that everyone plays with the same scorecard
- Learn a non-threatening, non-confrontational way of "keeping score"

PART 5: RELATIONSHIPS

If your family has a clear vision, has unity around that vision, manages the macro and micro systems that govern your daily life, and tracks key metrics, your relationships are bound to improve. Nonetheless, relationships are the trickiest part of this mortal life. Each person has a God-given temperament and unique personality. In the corporate world, we have made great headway in leading people and collaborating with them according to their natural strengths. We ought to do the same with the family.

Tools included:

- The Relationship Maximizer™
- The Conflict Analyzer™

Do you ever feel like your most important relationships are in a rut? Are you ready to take them to the next level? Break free from the complexity holding you back. Our goal is to clarify your thoughts, emotions, and actions toward loved ones.

Learn your family's key personality traits.

- Determine which of the four Greek temperaments your family members possess
- Learn how to speak to and act toward each temperament
- Discover how to maximize any relationship: your relationship with God, a spouse, a child, a friend, or even an enemy
- Equip yourself to analyze a conflict immediately after it happens to understand what you and the other person were both thinking and feeling so that you are better prepared to handle the situation as your better self the next time it occurs

PART 6: DISCERNMENT

Every family has urgent and important decisions to make, whether it's what to feed the kids for dinner tonight or whether you should pick up and move to a new town. There's a difference between decision making and problem solving. Decision making has to do with choosing between multiple options, such as which family car to purchase. Problem solving is about figuring out the root cause of an issue.

Decision-making tools included:
- The Family Focus Box™
- The Family Pros and Cons List
- The Family CBA™
- The Family Decision Matrix™

Discernment is wisdom in action.
- Prioritize the urgent and important over the not-so-urgent and not-so-important
- Condition yourself to use the tried-and-true pros and cons list to get the issue out of your head and onto paper
- Weigh multiple alternatives against each other to find the best option according to your own standards

Problem-solving tools included:
- The Five Whys
- The 80/20 Family Optimizer™

To really solve a problem, you have to go beneath the surface and get to the heart of the issue.
- Get to the root cause of the problem by asking (like a little kid), "Why, why, why . . ."
- Optimize the vital few activities in your life that give you the vast majority of the benefits and eliminate the few negative things in life that cause most of the problems

There you have it. The six-part family management system. I hope the journey you are about to undertake is rewarding for you and your family. Remember, this *is* a journey. You do not create a well-ordered family in a day any more than you create a well-ordered business in a day. It takes time. It takes continuous improvement. But, my friend, you have far more power over how your family is structured and the good that your family pursues than you might realize.

My dad always says, "God may feed the birds, but He don't put the food in the nest." That's his folksy way of saying God will indeed bless you, but He expects you to do all within your power to build the foundation upon which His grace will flow.

By implementing these six principles in your family, you are creating a firm foundation. You may not find complete peace, but you will feel contentment. Most of all, your family will be far better equipped to receive the grace that God has in store for you.

PART-1

VISION

Vision

Unity

Metrics

WELL-ORDERED FAMILY

Systems

Relationships

Discernment

TM

"The best way to predict the future is to create it."

—PETER DRUCKER

"The best way to show that a stick is crooked
is not to argue about it or to spend time denouncing it,
but to lay a straight stick alongside it."

—SAINT FRANCIS DE SALES

1

BEING A VISIONARY

QUO VADIS?

There's an old Christian story about Simon Peter, Jesus's righthand man—also infamous as the disciple who cowardly denied his Lord three times before the cock crowed. Years later, Peter—who also happens to be the central leader of the early Christians, the first Pope, and the rock on which Jesus said he would build his Church—journeyed to Rome to minister to the young Christian community tenuously established there.

About this time, the economy and civil order began to go south for Nero, the current Roman emperor. Instead of righting his own ship, Nero cast about for someone to blame and lighted on that odd new religion that denied the Roman gods and ministered even to outcasts and slaves, that is, the early Christians. Thus began a terrible persecution that resulted in many deaths, and great suffering. Christian martyrdom was everywhere. In AD 65, at the height of this jackbooted attack on his flock, Peter decided to flee Rome and the troubles there. Was Peter experiencing a similar cowardice as he did thirty years before when he denied knowing Jesus three times? Was he being strategic by escaping death in order to continue his evangelization? We will never know. But what happened next seems to imply Peter was straying from his true mission.

Peter was hurrying along the Appian Way, the ancient Roman main road, heading south away from Rome when he suddenly saw the resurrected Jesus heading north toward Rome. Shocked, Peter asked, *"Domine, Quo vadis?"* (Lord, where are you going?) And Jesus answered, "I am going to Rome to be crucified again."

Well, that stopped Peter in his tracks. If Peter was not willing to face the persecution, then Jesus must do it Himself again? It was like a repeating nightmare! Was Peter to deny his Lord *again*?

The proper question was not "where are You going, Lord?"

The question, as Jesus demonstrated to his errant disciple, was "where are you going, *Peter*?"

Quo vadis?

And Peter knew in his heart there was only one answer. Head back to Rome, and to the persecution and possible death that awaited him there.

Why? Because there are some things more important than life and death. Some things have eternal consequences.

Peter was right about the persecution. Shortly after this scene on the Appian Way, he was crucified. According to the ancient story, he was nailed upon the cross upside down at his own request, for he felt unworthy to die in the same way as his Lord.

Peter turned back and faced the chaos, the evil, the dysfunction because he knew he had the one answer to it all.

Did his answer result in fields of sugar plums and daisies for Peter?

No. The opposite, in fact.

But it did result in fulfillment. Purpose. Eternal reward for Peter. Beyond that, Peter's decision resulted in the foundation of a church that would one day convert the Roman Empire to Christianity and bring God's truth to a broken world. Although he didn't live to see it and possibly never expected it, Peter's vision would one day become Rome's vision. Rome would become a Christian Empire. And the rest is history.

This Latin phrase, *Quo vadis*, is a way to ask: What are you doing with your life? What is your life purpose? What is your vocation? It's a beautifully simple way to create a vision for yourself and your family.

Remember those diagrams of a prism in your old science books from high school? The white light passes through a focal point and from there is split into beautiful, precise bands of color. Think of *Quo vadis* as your focal point, the place where the scatter of your family life can become coherent and, eventually, result in a rainbow.

It all starts with one simple question.

Ask yourself: Where is your family going? Are you just following the crowd? Are you blindly fleeing down the Appian Way of life with no objective in mind? Or will you define your destination with precision?

Every successful business spends hours upon hours honing, refining, and clarifying its vision: what it wants to be, where it wants to go, and why it's worth the effort.

If you were running a business, would you take the time to crystallize a vision? Would you do this to satisfy your customers, motivate your employees, and keep yourself from veering off track? Of course you would.

Why, then, would you not do this with your family? Why would you not do this with the eternal souls within your care?

Quo vadis?

VISION: MORE THAN JUST SEEING

Vision can be a tricky word. According to the Oxford English Dictionary, the first definition of vision is *the state of being able to see*. But it's the second definition where vision starts to get interesting: *the ability to think about the future with imagination or wisdom*.

Vision is the *why*. Why are you doing what you are doing? Why do you have faith? Why did you marry your spouse, take that job, have those kids? It is the *why* for the small things as well. Why do your kids play soccer or have cell phones? Why did you buy that car or make that charitable contribution? Why, why, why . . .

The more refined your vision is, the better you can make those important decisions *and* the small but urgent ones as well. With a proper vision, things fall into place.

THE VISIONARY

A third definition for vision is the most interesting: *an experience of seeing someone or something in a dream or trance, or as a supernatural apparition.* There is a mystical quality about it because you are looking to the future. You are envisioning qualities of your family they don't yet have. A business must envision skills and attributes that it doesn't yet possess. Long-term visions might even foresee technology that doesn't seem possible at the moment.

Every vision, however, must come from a visionary. That is you. It is your job and no one else's. You can't outsource the vision for your family. If you don't come up with a vision for your family, no one will. Don't see yourself in this role? Too bad. You've got it. Fortunately, you are not alone. I'm going to give you the tools and backup to handle it. We can start by realizing that you don't have to fit into a specific mold. All visionaries are not alike.

They come in many varieties. Moses was a visionary when he foresaw the Promised Land for the Chosen People. Great missionaries have envisioned the conversion of multitudes of people. Great explorers have envisioned distant lands and overcome great obstacles to reach their destinations. The Founding Fathers of the United States envisioned a unique form of government protected by inalienable rights. And most recently, great business visionaries have radically altered our world with technological advancement.

The greatest visionaries often see something that the average mind thinks is completely out of reach. Henry Ford envisioned every American being able to afford a car. Thomas Edison had the seemingly impossible idea of electricity in every household. Ray Kroc thought it was possible to get a burger, fries, and milkshake within seconds of ordering it. And Elon Musk is trying to figure out how to colonize Mars long before the technology exists to accomplish this. It is often the vision that gives birth to ingenuity.

Business is a wonderful place to see vision coming to fruition. But there is no reason why it can't be the same for family. In fact, it's a shame that many of these great corporate visionaries have no vision for their home life. It's an open secret that many famous visionaries had fractured and painful personal lives, with their ex-spouses and children becoming collateral damage in their headlong pursuit of greatness. Too bad they didn't see, or take the time, to apply that native genius to their most important relationships.

It is the job of mothers and fathers to devise clear visions for their families. Behavior that might seem impossible may be exactly what you are called to pursue. There's no rule that says you can't have a family of saints. There's no reason your family can't defy the odds. There's nothing that says your home can't be a place of joy, charity, and prayer. There is no reason that your children can't carry on your vision into future generations. Very often, the biggest hurdle keeping this from happening is a shallow vision that aims far too low, expects far too little, and accepts mediocrity. Imagine if Edison had settled for "good enough" in his laboratory. You'd be reading this book by candlelight.

I remember the first time I thought of myself as the visionary for my family. It was after I had fully embraced the title of "Visionary" at work. I had begun to appreciate it more than CEO because it was a title that gave me direction. CEO makes me an executive, but it doesn't tell me what duties I'm supposed to execute. Visionary does, and yet it gives me wiggle room to craft "vision work" to fit the needs of the different companies I oversee. And while others on my team contribute to the vision every day, I know that a carefully considered and clearly articulated vision for each company is ultimately my responsibility.

In my family life, my wife runs virtually every aspect of the day-to-day activities. For us (with fifteen kids), this includes homeschooling, managing the education that we outsource, paying the bills and keeping up with insurance companies, taking care of all medical issues and doctor appointments (every doctor and nurse thinks my wife has medical training when they speak to her), social activities for the kids, and feeding a ton of people multiple times a day! The list can go on and on. I would be a fool to come home from work and try to take over these areas. And yet, I am not a mere "special helper" for my wife. I am the husband and father. And to be very frank, I struggled mightily for quite some time to figure out the practical implications of this in my own home.

When I realized that I could and should be the Visionary for my family, I felt at peace. In our particular family it is my task to keep the big picture in mind, to ensure that our daily life is working toward our ultimate goals, to lead effective and peaceful discussion when things get off course, to incorporate our faith into our daily lives, and to inspire my wife and children toward the good, true, and beautiful.

Whether the Visionary role is embraced by one spouse or it's a shared responsibility, the main point is this: you must be intentional about crafting and protecting your family vision. Embrace this role. Take time to consider what it means. I know it can seem overwhelming at first. But imagine the places you can take your family! I guarantee you that the initial temporary discomfort will seem miniscule compared to the payoff on the follow through of your vision. And Well-Ordered Family™ has plenty of helpful tools to get you there.

WORKING *ON* AND *IN* THE FAMILY

You've probably heard how business leaders must work *on* their business rather than just *in* their business. What does this mean? As a CEO, I can tell you that this is harder than it sounds.

At work, it's common for someone to poke their head in my office and say, "Hey Conor, you got a minute?" It's the most misleading sentence in my professional life.

To be clear, the person isn't intentionally being deceptive. Probably. But you can bet your bottom dollar that whatever it is will certainly not take one minute. It might start an entire hour of discussion, trigger a whole day of work, or create a week's worth of mental effort.

Maybe it's a "little" accounting issue that prevents accurate reports, a technology issue that makes you look silly to customers, or a fragile personnel issue that has to be handled sensitively. "Hey Conor, you got a minute?" signals that I'm about to be pulled into working *in* the business when I would prefer to work *on* the business.

This is precisely why I have a home office. It's very hard to work *on* the business in the middle of all the daily operations. Most visionaries have a secret getaway place: the local library, Starbucks, or the old shed in the backyard repurposed into a home office. The psychologist Carl Jung had an unheated stone mini-castle perched on the edge of a mountain lake.[1]

---

1 Jung, C. G. *Memories, Dreams, Reflections.* New York: Vintage books, 1989. P. 223-227.

No matter where it is, you must get away to see the business from a holistic perspective, to see the most important issues, and to make the most important decisions. Working on the business is very much like Robin Williams in *Dead Poets Society* standing on his desk and looking at the classroom from a different angle. He convinces his students to do the same.

I'm not suggesting you get the kids to climb up on the furniture and refer to you only as "O Captain! My Captain!" but you do need to look at your family from a different perspective.

You spend most of your time working *in* the family: paying bills, cooking and cleaning, driving from one event to another, changing diapers, doing dishes and laundry, teaching grammar, teaching math, dealing with teachers, confiscating phones . . . the list never ends.

My house is no different. One of my greatest frustrations is that most conversations with my wife are interrupted by the kids. Usually, we attempt these conversations in the morning before I go to work. And inevitably, as you might imagine with fifteen kids, one kid after another cuts in: the babies pitch a fit, the middle kids need help with school, the teenagers want to discuss which car they are driving, even the adult kids are texting or calling asking for help or advice. And all I want is to have ten minutes to talk with my wife!

Ashley rolls with these interruptions like a pro, partly because she deals with it all day long. But part of me expects (unfairly so) that I should be free from interruptions at home because I am bombarded at the office with, "Hey Conor, got a minute?"

I know I must get away and think about the business. It is no different for family life. Ashley and I must get away and work *on* the family. And if we aren't intentional about this, it will never happen.

But what does working on the family mean? First, it doesn't mean going to dinner and just discussing the most recent logistics of family life. It isn't just talking about the kids when the kids aren't around. And it's not just making soft complaints about the list of things to do around the house.

Working *on* your family means discussing your long-term vision, checking how the core virtues are holding up, exploring ways to deepen your faith, monitoring the environments (macrosystems) through which your kids are maneuvering and coming up with ways to improve the daily processes (microsystems), updating the metrics by which you judge your success and hold each other accountable, examining the important relationship dynamics in the family, and discerning urgent and important issues.

I know this can seem like a lot at first, but with practice, you will learn to recognize when you are working *in* your family versus working *on* your family. The good news is that you don't have to necessarily work harder, just differently. The length or intensity of the conversation isn't the point. What matters most is the mindset you bring. Are you trying to stay one step ahead in the chaos of the day, or are you looking for systematic ways to improve your family life? Staying ahead of the chaos is working *in* the family; looking for a better system is working *on* it.

Well-Ordered Family™ is here to help you work *on* your family as simply as possible.

CHAPTER

2

THE

FAMILY MASTER PLAN™

By this point in your family life, you may have delved into creating chore charts. You may have created a family calendar. These are great, but you realize they aren't satisfying in and of themselves. Perhaps the meaning and purpose you want to feel as a family is eluding you.

Frustration sets in.

Quo vadis?

Where the heck am I going?

Where are *we* going?

Oh, I feel you. I've been there. More than once.

TEAM FRUSTRATION

Your typical CEO reaches a point of extreme frustration. The team seems to be on different pages. The department heads are not talking to one another. The products or services being offered lack cohesion. The CEO himself feels he is grasping at any business opportunity to grow revenue even as he experiences a nagging discomfort with going off mission. And so, out of desperation, he tries to *really* feel like a leader. He rents a beach house for the executive team, and they embark on a three-day strategic planning session. The CEO has each team prepare beautiful PowerPoint presentations that address their long-term plans, their budgetary needs for next year, and that provide a deep analysis of the key result areas.

By the time all is said and done, the team goes through thirty or more pages of information and pie charts and bar graphs. The CEO is impressed with everything from the colors on the PowerPoint to the polished presentations. He delegates his most trusted colleague to combine all of this information into a three-year strategic plan. Upon return to the real world, the trusted colleague makes another beautiful twelve-page plan, and even goes to Staples to get it nicely bound—one copy for each executive. The beautiful plan is plopped down on each person's desk . . .

Rests there for a few weeks . . .

And finally is quietly moved to the most prominent bookshelf in the office. A genuine position of honor!

Three years later, no one has opened it, and the plan is still sitting there.

While I won't pronounce such an exercise a complete waste of time, it is horrifically ineffective. Moreover, I've seen it happen time and time again. Why? Because I've been that CEO.

And then, I discovered a company called EOS, which stands for Entrepreneurial Operating System.[2] EOS mastered the art of simplifying business complexity. They have a one-page document that captures the most important aspects of the business's long-term and mid-term vision and goals. They call this the Vision/Traction Organizer®. A company that uses this one tool is lightyears ahead of our business described above. In most places in life, less is more. This is true for business, and it is definitely true for your family.

Many other business consulting firms have programs similar to EOS designed to simplify the complex. For example, I have benefited greatly not

---

2 "What Is Eos?" EOS Worldwide, May 31, 2023. https://www.eosworldwide.com/what-is-eos.

THE FAMILY MASTER PLAN™

Vision+ Statement:

Family Motto:

Family Beatitude:

Family Patron:

Core Virtues:

Strengths:

Weaknesses:

Three-Year Goals:

Opportunities:

Threats:

Ten-Year Portrait:

Family Signatures:

only from EOS but from Scaling Up,[3] Pinnacle,[4] and Strategic Coach.[5] Each has its own specialty and nuances. Strategic Coach, for example, is targeted at the CEO rather than the business. My point in mentioning these other businesses is this: my entire executive education has directly benefited my family life. I have adapted the concepts from organizing a long-term corporate vision to leading my family.

Just as in my businesses, I found that I could simplify my family's complicated life into one page, a page that I could continually point to when things got off track, a page that was aspirational but also practical.

The result was The Family Master Plan™.

The greatest benefit of working through the Family Master Plan is *not* the end result of having everything on one page; it is the process of forging the family into something stronger and more beautiful.

Now let's get to high value stuff—starting with The Family SWOT™.

THE FAMILY SWOT™

Etched above the entrance to the Oracle of Delphi was an axiom that resonates to this day: *Know Thyself.* Any planning process begins with self-discovery. Smart businesses use different tools to diagnose themselves.

A traditional SWOT analysis is probably the most widely used method for a business to get a grip on its identity. SWOT stands for Strengths, Weaknesses, Opportunities, and Threats. We can definitely apply SWOT to family life, as well. On the next page, you will see what The Family SWOT™ tool looks like.

Strengths and weaknesses have an internal origin. They come from within your family. Opportunities and threats, on the other hand, are of external

---

3 "Scaling up Performance Platform." Scaling Up. https://scalingup.com/.

4 Pinnacle Business Guides. https://pinnaclebusinessguides.com/.

5 "Premier Business Coach for Entrepreneurs: Strategic Coach." The Strategic Coach, November 10, 2023. https://www.strategiccoach.com/.

origin, coming from outside your family. We have included examples in the illustration, but below is a longer list of possibilities to consider.

You might have a totally different list. That's great! But here are some strengths and weaknesses to think about. Check those that apply to your family.

STRENGTHS	WEAKNESSES
☐ Humor	☐ Poor communication
☐ Physically active	☐ Lack of trust
☐ Enjoy time together	☐ Too much conflict
☐ Prayerful	☐ Dysfunctional logistics
☐ Fiscally responsible	☐ Unresolved issues
☐ Orderly	☐ Financial instability
☐ Strong emotional support	☐ Lack of empathy
☐ Effective communication	☐ Poor conflict resolution
☐ Resilience	☐ Inflexible
☐ Education/Academics	☐ Resentments
☐ Healthy and Fit	☐ Too much technology and media
☐ Strong social networks	☐ Lack of prayer
☐ Empathetic	☐ Lack of structure/daily routine
☐ Adaptable	☐ Too much anger

If you're like me, the stark reality of seeing how many weaknesses your family has can be depressing at first. Believe me, I understand! My wife and I are flooded with compliments regarding our children. "Your children behave so well in church," or "I'm amazed at how good your teenagers are with the little kids!" These are true. We are blessed with remarkably good and virtuous children. But you'd better believe they can show their nasty side at home. As the saying goes, familiarity breeds contempt. Our kids can duke it out with the best of them! And I (less so, my wife) am often on my worst behavior in the comfort of my own home. This may seem natural and understandable—but it's also unacceptable.

My family's most recent SWOT analysis (just a few weeks ago at the time of this writing) showed we have a weakness in charity, particularly in charitable tones of voice toward one another. Since working through The Family SWOT™ and discovering this about our own family, things have improved. Are they 100 percent better? No. But we can now *name* the problem when it comes up. We are attuned to it. And you can be too. But it requires a little discomfort to be honest with yourself and your family. Admitting a problem is always the first step in the healing process. Or, to put it more prosaically, if you want to get out of a hole, the first step is to stop digging.

Now that you've considered strengths and weaknesses within your family, let's shift our focus to the external factors that affect your family in positive and negative ways. Below is a lengthy list of opportunities your family may choose to pursue and a list of potential threats your family may face.

OPPORTUNITIES	THREATS
☐ New educational or career options	☐ Debt
☐ Getting involved with church groups	☐ Inflation
☐ Finding a better network of friends for teenagers	☐ Bad influence of friends
☐ Investments	☐ Too much cell phone use
☐ Better technology to cut down on cell phone abuse	☐ Improper sites or media consumption
☐ Celebrating family milestones	☐ Loss of income/job
☐ Scheduling a vacation	☐ Conflict with neighbors
☐ New hobbies	☐ Conflict with extended family
☐ More frequent reception of the sacraments at church	☐ Too many activities pulling us apart
☐ Cutting out activities	☐ Burnout

After determining the most significant strengths, weaknesses, opportunities, and threats, you can write them on The Family Master Plan™, which is the first step to building a great one-page summary for your family vision.

While we are skimming the surface at the moment, The Family SWOT™ is a good shortcut to get to perhaps the most important part of The Family Master Plan™, your Family Vision+ Statement.

THE FAMILY SWOT™

HELPFUL To Your Family

HARMFUL To Your Family

INTERNAL ORIGIN

Helpful:
We are humorous.
We have good routines.
We spend lots of time together.

Harmful:
We sometimes lack sensitivity.
We are too fast-paced.
Too much sibling conflict leads to parents lacking patience.

EXTERNAL ORIGIN

Helpful:
We have parish events.
We are friends with good families.
Homeschool co-op provides positive structure.

Harmful:
Technology creates mistrust and family conflict.
Too many activities decreases family time.
Financial stress creates conflict between Mom and Dad.

THE FAMILY VISION+ STATEMENT™

A vision statement for a traditional business concisely outlines the future state of an organization using minimal words. It's a long-term objective that serves as a guiding light during challenging times, reaffirming the ultimate goal. Typically encapsulated in a single sentence, it rep-

resents the essence of the business entity. As the adage suggests, "The main thing is to know the main thing and to keep the main thing the main thing." This principle holds true.

Take a look at the vision statements for some successful businesses.

- **LinkedIn:** Create economic opportunities for every member of the global workforce.
- **Southwest:** To be the world's most loved, most efficient, and most profitable airline.
- **IKEA:** To create a better everyday life for many people.
- **Tesla:** To create the most compelling car company of the 21st century by driving the world's transition to electric vehicles.

These memorable one-liners encapsulate the essence of each business. But they are more often than not a branding effort. They communicate the essence of the business to customers, in a simple (some would say simplistic) billboard-like manner. While this vision statement certainly serves as a motivator internally, it isn't enough for day-to-day operations. An employee needs more than that to be told to put his nose to the grindstone.

And so, while I love vision statements, I think families need something deeper, for the same reason employees need an authentic motivating factor. Families aren't advertising their brand in a short and sweet one-liner. When you have to sell furniture like Ikea, you need a sales pitch in as few words as possible. Families aren't in that line of business. Or any line of business.

At the same time, it is important for a family to be able to express the family vision toward one another in a concise way. The reason I believe families need more than just a one-liner is because we need a statement to encapsulate exactly how we are going to accomplish this vision. Without that extra "umph," we will be doomed to inhabit empty platitudes like, "The purpose of the Gallagher family is to get to heaven," or "The purpose of the Smith family is to love each other."

Okay. Great. Thank you. That might not be a bad *advertisement* for a family. But just as the internal team of a business needs more than that a vision statement to get to work in a particular way, a family requires more as well. Family life isn't a billboard. We need something authentic and specific to the entire life we lead. That's where the Family Vision+ Statement comes in.

The Family Vision+ Statement is an impactful one-liner accompanied by a few descriptive sentences. The idea is to put the essence of your family into words and then outline the approach you'll take to realize this vision. This Family Vision+ Statement will be your family's primary focus and serve to make sure nothing gets in the way of implementing it.

Language

Formulating a Family Vision+ Statement provides you with a chance to envision your family through the lens of how you aspire to be seen by God. The way to achieve this ideal is through tangible action steps. Start by completing one of the following introductory phrases.

- ☐ *The vision of the* _____ *Family is to . . ."*
- ☐ *"The mission of the* _____ *Family is to . . ."*
- ☐ *"The reason the* _____ *Family exists is to . . ."*
- ☐ *"The purpose of the* _____ *Family is to . . ."*
- ☐ *"God created the* _____ *Family in order to . . ."*
- ☐ *"God brought the* _____ *Family together in order to . . ."*

Now that you have an opening sentence, let's consider a few questions to help you nail down the remainder of your Family Vision+ Statement. You can jot down your answers right inside this book and transfer the finished draft onto your downloaded version of The Family Master Plan™.

Take the time to read the full draft multiple times. See if there is any way to clarify it. The shorter and cleaner, the better. Now, in the space provided on page 33, write your official full and complete Family Vision+ Statement.

THE FAMILY VISION+ STATEMENT BUILDER™	
1 **GOALS & OBJECTIVES**	**2** **"THE HOW"**
List the long-term goals that your family hopes to accomplish.	Now, in the most practical sense, how is your family going to accomplish these goals? List 3-5.
Closer relationships within the family. Gain stronger devotion and piety. Peaceful home with minimal conflict.	Keep Sunday as a family day. Volunteer to help vs. waiting to be asked. Each kid gets more one-on-one time with Mom and Dad.
3 **BEGINNING**	**4** **FULL DRAFT**
Draft your first sentence. This is supposed to be broad and idealistic.	Take your first sentence and connect it to your "Hows." This will make your idealistic goal a practical goal.
God created the Smith family to show the beauty and joy of the Christian life.	God created the Smith family to show the beauty and joy of the Christian life. We aim to achieve this by serving one another, by keeping Sunday as a family day, and by intentionally cultivating our relationships.

The Official _____ **Family Vision+ Statement**

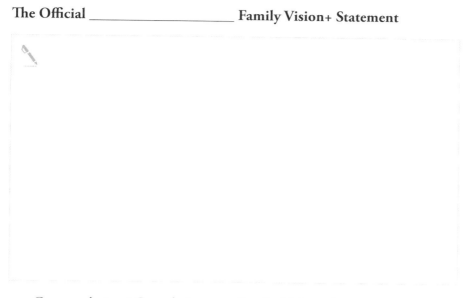

Congratulations! Completing your Family Vision+ Statement is a big step to sustaining and supercharging your progress toward a Well-Ordered Family.

CORE VIRTUES

The business world speaks about Core Values. In the realm of family, I propose embracing Core *Virtues* rather than Core Values. The difference is subtle but significant. Values tend to be highly subjective, varying from person to person. Just as beauty is native to the individual viewpoint, value is in the eye of the beholder. For instance, my appreciation for poached eggs, modern art, or Shakespeare's Coriolanus may differ from yours. So may the value I place on playing golf on Wednesday, or driving a sensible Ford. Opinions about these things are not right or wrong in any permanent sense. They're subjective.

By contrast, virtues have timeless and objective qualities. They are built in to human nature. In fact, I believe they are built into the universe itself. Purity and prudence, for instance, remain virtues regardless of culture or era. I encourage your family to engage in discussions and prioritization of virtues over mere values. Leonardo da Vinci said, "Who sows virtue reaps honor."

No Scorekeeping

In my own family, "No Scorekeeping" is a Core Virtue we embrace to counteract the temptation to tally chores and privileges. Pretty much on a daily basis, one kid has to cover for another. Jude will be at basketball practice and not be available to do dishes. So, I look around the room for some other kid to step into the breach. By this point, they know what I am doing. They are ducking and hiding so I don't choose them.

I'll see the ten-year-old trying to slip upstairs and out of sight. *Gotcha!*

"David. I need you to step up, man. Come on."

"But Jude never helps me with my chores. And I took care of the chickens and goats for Teresa last night when she was gone."

"No scorekeeping, David."

He may slouch his shoulders and grumble, but he trundles back downstairs.

"No scorekeeping" is a shortcut to the virtues of generosity and humility. I don't want to have a catechism lesson every day. So, I try to find shortcuts.

But sometimes when my shortcut explanation fails, I'll really lay it on thick. I'll call my kids into the room and proclaim, "Do any of my beloved children volunteer to be a Christian right now?" Which is a kind of shortcut of its own.

Sure, I'm not fighting fair. Or am I?

Could guilt be the ultimate shortcut to communication!

The point is to urge you to explore unique and imaginative expressions for your family's Core Virtues. Being able to articulate what these are helps immensely when the chaos of everyday life seems to be getting the better of you.

Another example of a shortcut phrase I have begun using with my kids is what I call "AS we." What is it?

When I was at the Franciscan University of Steubenville, the president of my school, Father Michael Scanlon, gave a series of one-line homilies. Short sermons certainly bolstered chapel attendance. On this particular day, the Gospel reading was the place where Christ teaches His disciples the Lord's Prayer. Everyone sat still to the end of the Gospel anticipating the one-liner.

Father Scanlon held the silence in the air masterfully. The suspense built in the sanctuary and most certainly in my heart. And then, with a deep and passionate voice, he bellowed out "*AAASSS* we!"

The word "as" echoed off the walls and penetrated every person listening. Father Scanlon stared at us for a moment, and took his seat.

What in the world, I asked myself. Did Father Scanlon just yell "ass" in Church?

No, that couldn't be it.

We all sat in silence for what seemed like an hour.

"As we . . . As we . . . As we . . ."

My mind turned the phrase over and over again. Finally the explanation hit me. It was right there in the prayer.

"Forgive us our trespasses *as we* forgive those who trespass against us."

I realized that I had been asking the Father to forgive my sins in the same way, and to the same extent, that I forgave other's sins against me.

That is, begrudgingly. Or, to tell the truth, really not at all.

Oh crap, I thought. I'm asking God to treat *me* as *I* treat others. And the way I treat others could, to say the least, stand a great deal of improvement. It often was downright deplorable.

We'd better *hope* God does not forgive us *as we* forgive others most of the time, or there would be no forgiveness at all.

Since then, the Lord's Prayer does not rattle so easily from my tongue. When I hit the "as we," I quail at my own neglect of others.

Jesus's model prayer comes with its own builtin rebuke of our own self-righteousness and ill treatment of others—along with a coach's challenge to do better.

Most of the scorekeeping in my house occurs over a perceived injustice.

It is Imelda's turn to swap out the chickens' water, but David has been asked to it.

The teenagers have been gone every night this week and didn't do any of their chores on the chore chart, so Teresa and Annie get stuck doing the dishes multiple nights in a row.

The six-year-old twins are keeping score over who got stuck in the far back of the van the most in the last few days.

Perhaps even Ashley and I keep score over who had the sourest attitude over the past few days.

It's time to pull out an "AS we."

Or consider this. A *bam* echoes from upstairs followed by the cries of an outraged kid. The sound of padding feet. Someone comes down to say "He hit me with that wooden block right in the head!"

I've learned to immediately inquire, "And what did you do to cause that?"

"Nothing! I didn't do anything!"

"Oh really! Your six-year-old brother just decided out of thin air to hit you in the head with a block, huh?"

So, you investigate and, sure enough, the victim was also the instigator. Maybe she had been poking fun at her brother for the previous ten minutes. Maybe she had willfully stepped on him as she walked by. Yet it was done behind the scenes and it was sneaky, and she masterfully wears a look of innocence.

Of course it isn't justified to retaliate with a block to the head, either. So, like fathers from time immemorial, I punish both kids.

Oh, the incredulous tones!

"What? *Why*? I didn't do anything wrong!"

At such times, it's helpful to have trained the little one in the "AS we" shorthand of life.

I don't want him to just fear retaliating because it might make me mad. I want him to fear retaliating because he wants ultimately to be forgiven by God for his own offenses.

Can I explain this to every child in every single instance? There's a one-way ticket to absolute exhaustion.

But I can catch my kid's gaze and say, "*AAASSS* we," just like Father Scanlon said to me those twenty-five years ago.

Discovering Your Family's Core Virtues

Your family possesses a unique essence, making certain Core Virtues resonate deeply. These virtues encapsulate the essence of your family and are what you desire God to see in your family above all else. Yet you are not God. You are timebound and you don't always see the complete picture. It is important to acknowledge that these Core Virtues can evolve over time as your family grows and your children mature. They are not set in stone.

THE FAMILY CORE VIRTUES BUILDER™

Behaviors to Increase	How To Decrease	
What are the behaviors that bring joy and peace to your family?	Primary Obstacles:	Unique Opportunity:
• Evening prayer as a family. • Older siblings helping and playing with little ones. • Sunday family brunch.	Older kids have too many activities that take away from family time.	Our family is good at scheduling and sticking to our commitments.

Behaviors to Increase	How To Decrease	
What are the behaviors that bring joy and peace to your family?	Primary Obstacles:	Unique Opportunity:
• Tattling on siblings. • Keeping score. • Back-talk.	Lack of humility.	Siblings are friends and enjoy spending time together.

Your Family's Core Virtues

Reflect on refining your lists of traits. Do you see commonalities?
Can you create your own word or phrase that resonates with your family in a special way?

1. Contentedness - Less complaining because I recognize my blessings clearly.

2. Proactiveness - Mom doesn't have to manage everything on a daily basis. The kids volunteer to help out.

3. Humility - This will cause us to desire to serve others above ourselves.

THE FAMILY CORE VIRTUES BUILDER™

Behaviors to Increase
What are the behaviors that bring joy and peace to your family?

-
-
-

How To Decrease

Primary Obstacles:	Unique Opportunity:

Behaviors to Increase
What are the behaviors that bring joy and peace to your family?

-
-
-

How To Decrease

Primary Obstacles:	Unique Opportunity:

Your Family's Core Virtues
Reflect on refining your lists of traits. Do you see commonalities?
Can you create your own word or phrase that resonates with your family in a special way?

1.

2.

3.

FAMILY MOTTO

Every great business has a powerful one-liner that grabs the heart of the customer. Imagine having a Family Motto that is just as powerful for the family members. Ask yourself: What is the one statement you want repeated over and over again in your home? What is that one phrase that's just right in good times and in bad? Think of the Family Motto as a weapon that your children can pull out in the darkest hour of spiritual warfare and in their moments of glory.

It could be a Scripture passage, a quote from a great saint or historical figure, or a phrase that you craft yourself. To help you discover your perfect Family Motto, we will look at some famous corporate taglines and the personal mottos of numerous famous people.

Corporate Taglines

A corporate tagline or slogan captures the essence, values, and distinctive qualities of a company in a concise and memorable manner. It plays a crucial role in marketing by setting the company apart from competitors. A great tagline remains etched in the customer's memory, leaving a lasting impression. In just a few words, a strong tagline powerfully communicates the company's core message and often inspires action. It is alluring and captivating. Once a company discovers its ideal tagline, it eagerly showcases it, proudly proclaiming, "This is who we are," and aims for widespread recognition.

When evaluating corporate taglines, try to not focus on whether you like this or that one, but recognize the brilliance of the short, sticky, and impactful phrase.

- **Nike:** "Just do it."
- **Apple:** "Think Different."
- **Coca-Cola:** "Open Happiness."
- **McDonald's:** "I'm Lovin' It."

Personal Mottos

A personal motto is a concise phrase embodying an individual's guiding principles, values, or mission. It acts as a mantra, reflecting his sense of purpose and influencing his choices and behaviors. It represents the essence of his core identity.

The greatest personal mottos have endured because they succinctly capture the defining attributes of singular individuals. Note that the people who said these words didn't sit down and craft their own personal motto. They are often simple statements that unintentionally became mottos due to their perfect alignment with the person's character, becoming inseparable from his identity. While these people may not have proclaimed these as their mottos, they did find themselves repeating them over and over again. Why? Because they wanted to push this particular message to those around them.

- **Socrates:** "Know thyself."
- **Julius Caesar:** "Veni, vidi, vici." (I came, I saw, I conquered.)
- **Marcus Aurelius:** "Memento mori." (Remember, you are mortal.)
- **Leonardo da Vinci:** "Simplicity is the ultimate sophistication."
- **Winston Churchill:** "Never give in, never, never, never, never."

Personally, I'm inspired by the spiritual examples of great saints.

- **Saint Teresa of Calcutta (Mother Teresa):** "Do something beautiful for God." Another motto applied to Mother Teresa is "Love until it hurts."
- **Saint Francis of Assisi:** "Pax et Bonum." (Peace and Goodness.)
- **Saint Ignatius of Loyola:** "Ad maiorem Dei gloriam." (For the greater glory of God.)
- **Saint Teresa of Ávila:** "Nada te turbe, nada te espante." (Let nothing disturb you, let nothing frighten you.)
- **Saint Thomas Aquinas:** "Contemplata aliis tradere." (To hand on to others the fruits of one's contemplation.)

Scripture Possibilities

"You shall know the truth and the truth will set you free!" (John 8:32)

I prefer Family Mottos that come directly from the Word of God. But your family is your own. The spirit may move you to something completely different. Just in case you are inclined toward finding a Family Motto from Scripture, here are a few examples from the Old and New Testaments that resonate with me as potential Family Mottos.

OLD TESTAMENT	NEW TESTAMENT
"The Lord is my strength and my praise" (Exodus 15:2).	"A new commandment I give unto you: That you love one another, as I have loved you, that you also love one another" (John 13:34).
"But as for me and my house, we will serve the Lord" (Joshua 24:15).	"Always rejoice" (1 Thes. 5:16).
"The Lord is my shepherd, and I shall want nothing" (Psalm 22:1).	"Pray without ceasing" (1 Thes. 5:17).
"I will praise the Lord at all times" (Psalm 33:2).	"Whatsoever you do to the least of my brethren, you do unto me" (Matthew 25:40).
"Be still, and see that I am God" (Psalm 45:11).	"Believe in the Lord Jesus, and you will be saved, you and your household" (Acts 16:31).

Crafting Your Family Motto

Your Family Motto serves as an expression of everything you have discerned thus far, a concise phrase that encapsulates your Vision, Core Virtues, significant goals, objectives, or qualities you aim to cultivate within your family over time.

1. Write down a few Family Motto contenders, those that have come to mind or popped off the page at you.
2. Next to each contender, jot down ways your family could use the motto in day-to-day life.

On the following page are a few blank spaces for you.

THE FAMILY MOTTO MAKER™	
MOTTO CONTENDER	**WAYS YOUR FAMILY COULD USE THIS MOTTO**

After prayerful consideration and discussion with your family, choose your Family Motto, write it below, and transfer it over to The Family Master Plan™.

The _____ Family Motto:

_____

FAMILY PATRON[6]

A Family Patron is a special guardian or protector chosen by a family to provide spiritual support and intercede on their behalf with God. In the Catholic faith, we often call these Patron Saints. They serve as inspiration and role models, offering guidance and prayers. But you don't have to be Catholic to choose a patron. It's a great way to embody the virtues that most resonate with you and your family. I just hope you don't choose the Emperor Palpatine or Genghis Khan.

The Role of a Family Patron

The Family Patron plays a crucial role in various aspects of family life. For Catholics, when the family experiences a sense of discord or imbalance, it is an opportune moment to call upon the Family Patron, those holy men and women in heaven, to help you during your earthly pilgrimage. They possess a

---

6 Biblical figures can certainly play this role. Perhaps Moses or John the Baptist really inspires your family. Great! Maybe the conversion of Mary Magdalene or St. Paul rings true in your life. Wonderful! You might prefer to choose a Family Hero/Role Model instead of a Family Patron. The goal is to choose someone family members can aspire to be like and draw inspiration from.

deeper understanding of what is amiss and, through their intercession, actively work toward restoring harmony while you focus on family responsibilities.

We seek the intercession of the Family Patron for protection, guidance, healing, unity, or defense against negative influences. But Catholic or not, invoking a Family Patron can be beneficial to concentrate the mind and heart, whether it's for resolving marital conflicts, addressing issues with teenagers, or dealing with illnesses circulating within the household. But remember, it isn't about being relieved of some suffering but rather learning to suffer as well as the holy men and women who have gone before us. They serve as examples because they are human beings like us who managed to live great and meaningful lives in the midst of a broken world.

Choosing the Patron: My Personal Story

Choosing a Family Patron can be a more complex decision than expected. Let me share my experience:

Initially, I filled out The Family Master Plan™ on my own, assuming Saint Joseph would be our patron. However, when I involved the family, one of our young children unexpectedly suggested Mother Teresa. At first, I thought it was because we have a picture of her in our house. But I was wrong. "Because she changed a lot of diapers!" our little girl said. That simple statement made it clear Mother Teresa was the perfect patron for our family, considering our current stage.

The moral of the story is that involving family members, especially children, in this decision is vital. They often offer unique insights. Furthermore, it's okay for the Family Patron to change over time, reflecting different family dynamics.

Whether you stick with one patron or change annually, both approaches are beautiful. Imagine dedicating a year to learning about and developing a personal relationship with a different saint or figure of faith and virtue. Regularly reviewing your Family Master Plan can help you assess if a change is needed—guided by the Holy Spirit if you are a Christian.

Examples of categories include patrons of marriage, children, sickness and healing, special needs, workers,

CATEGORY	DESCRIPTION	EXAMPLE PATRONS
Patrons of Leaders	These patrons demonstrate a deep love for others, courage, and confidence in their own abilities, inspiring others to follow them.	☐ Moses ☐ King David
Patrons of Wisdom	These patrons serve as an example of humility, trustworthiness, and accountability in making wise decisions.	☐ Solomon ☐ Daniel
Patrons of Children	These patrons are invoked for the well-being, education, and guidance of children within a family.	☐ St. Nicholas ☐ St. Maria Goretti
Patrons of Forgiveness and Reconciliation	These patrons represent forgiveness and healing broken relationships. They can help heal family rifts.	☐ St. Pope John Paul II ☐ St. Maximillian Kolbe
Patrons of Media and Technology	These patrons protect and guide families in responsible technology use, intercede for online safety, and promote balance in the digital age.	☐ St. Gabriel the Archangel ☐ St. Maximillian Kolbe
Patrons of Evangelization	These patrons exemplify evangelistic fortitude, sharing the message of faith in their communities on varying scales.	☐ St. Paul ☐ St. Patrick
Patrons of Hope and Perseverance	These patrons embody virtues of hope, resilience, and perseverance. They offer encouragement and strength during family challenges.	☐ St. Jude the Apostle ☐ St. Josephine Bakhita

education, forgiveness and reconciliation, media and technology, and so on. Don't limit your thinking to just "patrons of families." Your family has its own unique needs at this unique time. The canon of saints and biblical figures provide countless options for you to explore.

List the top three patrons that come to mind and share what aspect of each patron resonates with your family.

After prayerful consideration and group discussion, you can now choose your Family Patron.

Top 3:   **Why:**

_____   _____

_____   _____

_____   _____

The _____ Family Patron is _____ .

Before you finish this task, please keep in mind that each year you should consider as a family whether to choose a different patron for the new year. One of the many benefits of switching to a new patron each year is that you have only twelve months to get to know this saint. The time constraint motivates you to learn about his or her life and to invoke your patron's help more frequently. As silly as it sounds, consider having something tantamount to a Wall of Fame in your house where you add pictures of your patrons each year. Imagine ten or even twenty years down the road: you would have an incredible walk down memory lane, just as you do with family photos.

FAMILY BEATITUDE

Despite the fact that my oldest son is a professional umpire, I myself hate being an umpire in family feuds. This is not a competition anybody wins.

Every parent of two children knows what this is like. A pair, a group, a gaggle come running up to you and proceed to tell different stories, like a plaintiff and defendant before a judge.

No matter the issue, the phrases "Yes, you did!" "No, I didn't!" "Yes, you did!" "No, I didn't!" eventually spill out.

And I'm sitting there having no idea what the real truth is.

Actually, scratch that. I know the real truth.

The real truth is that neither of the children is living according to the Beatitudes.

Years ago, when my oldest were little guys, I grew tired of being asked to umpire. One day I literally held a trial at my dinner table. I sat at the table and I made the two kids who were fighting present their cases. The issue happened to involve two of the older kids. I had the little ones sit on the jury. I made the plaintiff and defendant prepare their case for about twenty minutes while I gave jury instructions to the little guys.

I think my youngest juror was four years old at the time. The babies were our spectators. Well, more like hecklers, really.

The plaintiff argued his case, the defendant made his. One of them called a witness (who happened to be on the jury at the same time).

It was chaotic. It was kind of fun for all. And I was rather pleased with the due process. The jury found for plaintiff. And then to mix things up (and certainly to mix up civil and criminal law), I had the jury issue a sentence.

The defendant would have to clean the playroom all . . . by . . . himself.

Sentenced to Alcatraz.

While this was an entertaining proceeding, I obviously could not put on a mock trial night after night.

Reflecting on this at the time, I found myself saying to our makeshift courtroom, "You know guys, this whole thing would be a lot easier if we just had one single peacemaker. That's all we would need to avoid all of this."

And at that moment, the most frequent of my paternal axioms was born: "Can I get a peacemaker?"

Blessed are the peacemakers, Jesus said. We take this very seriously in our house.

I have chosen to include the Beatitudes in The Family Master Plan™ for one simple reason: Jesus Christ will use the Beatitudes as *His* scorecard for our behavior.

Later we'll discuss the nature of a corporate scorecard and how you can create one for your own family. I believe Jesus is doing that right now with each of us. All manner of Christians believe that receiving salvation does not mean we can do whatever we please. It means we feel deep gratitude and strive to do God's will and please Christ. He sees every good and bad thing we do. What are *His* metrics? What are those standards of "success" He is using?

I can be pretty sure it isn't my most recent BMI, the balance in my 401k, the number of Our Fathers I have rattled off, or the number of kids I have had. It isn't even the number of people I have helped to convert!

No. It is the Beatitudes.

The Beatitudes were given to us in the greatest sermon ever given, the Sermon on the Mount. Of all the things ever written on living the Christian life, all the poetry and scriptural commentary, all the speculative theology and catechetical tools, the Beatitudes summarize the way of Christ more than any other.

The word "beatitude" means *blessed*, *happy*, or even *rich*. Jesus is telling you and me, your family and my own, that if we want to be blessed, happy, or spiritually rich, we must live according to these eight simple rules of life.

Beatitude Recap

Just in case it has been a while since you thought about the Beatitudes, here they are. I have placed the following into a chart so that you can see not only the beatitude, but the second part of the beatitude, or "the promise." I added a corresponding virtue related to each beatitude, the general meaning of each beatitude, and finally, a  family application. Read through the Beatitudes chart and search for a beatitude that applies to your family in a special way.

Talk with the family about which beatitude would bring the greatest sense of relief into your household right now. Go through a discussion process to narrow it down to a few. Then, write down or discuss how your top contenders could be used as a reminder of what virtues your family is striving for.

When you have a final decision on your Family Beatitude, transfer it over to The Family Master Plan™.

Our Family Beatitude is

BEATITUDE	PROMISE	VIRTUE	GENERAL MEANING	FAMILY APPLICATION
Blessed are the poor in spirit,	for theirs is the kingdom of heaven.	Humility	Humility and recognition of our need for God's grace	Teach children gratitude for what they have, prioritize service to others over material possessions, and seek spiritual growth together.
Blessed are the meek,	for they shall inherit the earth.	Gentle-ness	Gentleness and non-aggressive strength	Encourage peaceful communication, resolve conflicts calmly, promote empathy and understanding, and model humility and respect for others.
Blessed are they who mourn,	for they shall be comforted.	Compas-sion	Comfort in times of grief and loss	Support one another during times of grief, and offer consolation and support.
Blessed are they who hunger and thirst for righteousness,	for they shall be satisfied.	Justice	Righteous-ness and a desire for justice.	Foster a thirst for justice, act with integrity, promote fairness and compassion within the family, and strive for moral and ethical living.
Blessed are the merciful,	for they shall obtain mercy.	Mercy	Forgiveness and compassion toward others	Teach forgiveness and kindness. Don't let the kids keep score over silly little things. Show mercy and understanding and cultivate a spirit of compassion.

BEATITUDE	PROMISE	VIRTUE	GENERAL MEANING	FAMILY APPLICATION
Blessed are the pure of heart,	for they shall see God.	Purity	Sincerity and purity of intention	Encourage honesty and authenticity. No masks. Teach your kids that sincerity is better than insecure posturing.
Blessed are the peace-makers,	for they shall be called sons of God.	Charity	Reconcil-iation and harmony in relationships	Teach your kids to lose the arguments out of charity, for the "first shall be last" and "the last shall be first."
Blessed are they who suffer per-secution for justice's sake,	for theirs is the kingdom of heaven.	Fortitude	Perseverance and finding strength in times of adversity	Teach resilience in the face of challenges, support one another during difficult times, find strength in faith, and grow through suffering.

THE TEN-YEAR FAMILY PORTRAIT™

Perhaps the most influential business mind of the last twenty years is Jim Collins, author of *Good to Great*[7] and many other masterful works. One of the many influential concepts attributed to Collins is the BHAG—Big Hairy Audacious Goal.

Great businesses look deep into the future—ten to twenty-five years—and choose a lofty, ambitious goal that is awe-inspiring, motivating, and exciting. The quintessential BHAG was announced by President John F. Kennedy when he famously set a BHAG for the entire country: to put a man on the moon within a decade.

---

7 Collins, James C. *Good to Great: Why Some Companies Make the Leap ... and Others Don't.* New York, NY: Collins, 2009.

See It and Believe It

One primary reason that a BHAG or other long-term goals are so helpful for a business is that they invoke visualization. Visualization is a powerful tool in any aspect of life. It applies in business, relationships, and even sports. Several experiments have been performed in which test subjects who had never shot a basketball were handed the ball, put on the foul line, and asked to shoot away. The other half were asked to visualize shooting for a few minutes *before* they were handed the ball.[8] Not surprisingly, this latter group outperformed the first by a significant extent. Why? Because the human mind is powerful enough to steer the body into motion in very particular ways. Whether we are visualizing landing on the moon or shooting a foul shot, the mind's ability to see the upcoming event is one of the best methods to direct behavior thereafter.

While businesses can measure their success succinctly with singular goals, families are different. There is not one accomplishment for a family that sums up success (unless you consider an eternal reward of Paradise). So, what can the family envision?

I call this The Ten-Year Family Portrait™. Imagine what your life will look like in ten years: your age and the age of those around you, your job and financial status, your health and fitness, your spiritual state and prayer routine, your hobbies, you can even envision reconciliation with those who are estranged. There is so much you can envision that no single page can capture it all.

The Practical Side of Life

When I first looked ten years ahead with my family several years ago, it dawned on me that I would likely be a grandfather by then. What was even more shocking was that my beautiful wife would be a grandmother! *That* was hard for me to imagine. But that is the reality of my older kids moving on to their next phase in life and getting married. In just a few short years,

---

8 C.f. Grouios, George, Klio Semoglou, Katerina Mousikou, and Konstantinos Chatzinikolaou. "The Effect of a Simulated Mental Practice Technique on Free Throw Shooting Accuracy of Highly Skilled Basketball Players." Journal of Human Movement Studies 33(3):119-138, January 1997. https://www.researchgate.net /publication/331928345_The_effect_of_a_simulated_mental_practice_technique_on_free_throw_shooting _accuracy_of_highly_skilled_basketball_players.

what was a distant concept has become a reality. At the time of this writing, my oldest daughter is expecting our first grandchild. The Ten-Year Family Portrait™ has helped me focus on preparing my older kids to become parents themselves. And it sure makes me treasure the few short years I have left with the teenagers before they move on to the next stage of life. When the kids are little, you think you have all the time in the world, but you don't. Visualization helps keep the mind rooted in reality: your kids are growing up and leaving, your parents are aging and dying, and you and your spouse are growing old together. What does this mean to you?

In the space provided below, make some notes about the practical side of your life in ten years. Consider ages, stages of life, work and education, and maybe even finances. We will get to the intangibles below. For now, stick to the tangibles.

God's View

You don't have to pretend to know every aspect of your life ten years from today. There are so many unknowns. But I would encourage you to prayerfully consider not merely the tangible attributes of your family in a decade from now, such as age and money, but the intangibles, like character, spiritual attributes, and personal habits.

How do you want God to see your family ten years from today? Try to see yourself through God's eyes. What God will be looking at in ten years? What *should* He be looking at?

In the space below, write down the attributes of your family that you hope to develop in the next decade, particularly those that you believe would make God proud.

The Family

We have considered the practical side of life and the attributes that God wants to see develop in your family. But remember, we are not doing an individual portrait for each member of the family. It may have been helpful to think about each family member, but the goal of this exercise is to draft a family portrait of everyone at once. We are trying to describe what the family will look like as a group, not just a conglomerate of individuals.

Consider thinking about what activities the family can do together in ten years. Consider regular things you can do to stay in touch, to keep family unity, to deepen your relationships even if you physically move apart.

- Keep Sunday a family day for those in the area
- Have a weekly Zoom call with family that has moved away
- Have more one-on-one time for husband and wife
- Read one book, like a book club, each year together
- Hold your Annual Family Council session (more on that below)

Now make a few notes about how your family intends to grow and flourish. Try to picture what a beautiful version of your family will look like ten years from today.

Conclusion

It is now time to look over your notes above and to draft, in a very short sentence, the most important points of a ten-year portrait. The space provided on The Family Master Plan™ is intentionally small. Brevity is your friend. It is the only way for your family members to remember the gist of it. In fact, the content of The Family Master Plan™ should fit on one page. So, you really have to tighten up your version of The Ten-Year Family Portrait™.

In the spaces provided on the following page, you can make a few drafts. With each draft, try to shorten it. Hone it to its essence. When you've got it, transfer it over to your version of The Family Master Plan™.

Draft 1

Draft 2

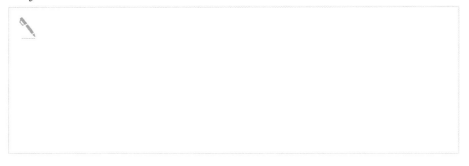

THREE-YEAR HOUSEHOLD GOALS

The final part of The Family Master Plan™ is to produce a short list of household goals to cover the next three years. You may be wondering why we set three-year goals after previously setting ten-year goals. How much goal-setting do you need, after all? But this is a good rule to follow, and I'll tell you why.

Notice that we began by setting a vision for you family. You might also consider this to be a lifetime goal. Then we painted a vivid picture of what your family might look like in ten years. But now it's time to draw a bit closer to our day-to-day life by setting three-year household goals. Goal setting is all about *beginning with the end in mind* (as Steven R. Covey made famous in his *7 Habits of Highly Effective People*[9]), and working backwards to today.

Given that we are focused on having a well-ordered family, it is helpful to articulate these three-year goals as "household" goals. Up to this point, a lot of our vision work has been more ethereal or conceptual. A three-year goal allows us to choose concrete, practical goals that are within sight.

In the Gallagher family, our family vision involves helping each other fulfill our vocations.

Great. But what about getting a car paid off? What about getting our kids in to college? What about our college kids receiving a strong launch into their careers? These are pretty darn practical.

There are also more tangible tasks that often take a great deal of effort over an extended period of time.

- Get a home garden up and running
- Build an outdoor shed for extra storage
- Replace the fence around the backyard
- Turn the front yard from weeds to grass
- Have all eligible family members become first-aid certified
- Create a stockpile of non-perishable food, and so on.[10]

Now it's time to establish Three-Year Household Goals that involve the entire family, aligning with the projects you may have around the home. Embrace this opportunity to seek your children's and spouse's support and contribution. Be open and transparent about where you need their assistance, fostering a sense of unity and shared responsibility within your family. While I have given examples and will provide more, only you can know the most important three-year goals for your family.

---

9 Covey, Stephen R. *The 7 Habits of Highly Effective People: 30th Anniversary Edition*. New York, NY: Simon & Schuster, 2020.

10 For those you who want to prep for something like "the grid going down", there are countless examples here: install solar panels, invest in a backup generator, learn basic survival skills, stockpile non-perishable foods, develop a plan for communication and meeting points in case of an emergency, establish a network for support and resources, learn to purify water, and so on.

GET S.M.A.R.T.

S.M.A.R.T. goals are a framework for setting effective and actionable objectives. The acronym S.M.A.R.T. stands for Specific, Measurable, Achievable, Relevant, and Time-Bound.

- **Specific:** Goals are clear and well-defined, focusing on a specific outcome. They answer the questions of what, why, and how.
- **Measurable:** Goals include measurable criteria to track progress and determine success. This allows for objective assessment and helps you stay motivated.
- **Achievable:** Goals are realistic and attainable. They stretch you but are still within reach. Setting achievable goals promotes confidence and prevents frustration.
- **Relevant:** Goals align with overall objectives, values, and aspirations. They are meaningful and relevant to your current situation and desired outcomes.
- **Time-Bound:** Goals have a defined timeframe for completion. This adds a sense of urgency and helps prioritize actions. Setting deadlines creates a sense of accountability and keeps you on track.

By following the S.M.A.R.T. framework, you can transform vague aspirations into concrete goals that are specific, measurable, achievable, relevant, and time-bound. This approach enhances clarity, increases motivation, and improves the likelihood of successful goal attainment.

S.M.A.R.T. Family Goals

Setting S.M.A.R.T. goals is a valuable approach when establishing three-year family goals. By applying the S.M.A.R.T. criteria to family aspirations, you can ensure that the goals are well-defined, realistic, and time-bound.

For example, a specific family goal could be to establish a weekly family mealtime routine. This goal is measurable because it can be tracked by the number of meals shared each week. It is achievable since it is within the family's control and resources. The relevance lies in fostering meaningful connections and open communication. Lastly, it's time-bound due to the three-year timeframe to establish and sustain the routine.

Another S.M.A.R.T. goal could be to create a dedicated family prayer space in your home within the next twelve months. This goal is specific, measurable (by designing and setting up the space), achievable with proper planning, relevant to strengthening spirituality, and time-bound within twelve months.

By setting S.M.A.R.T. goals, families can effectively outline their intentions, track progress, stay motivated, and work together toward achieving meaningful objectives over a three-year timeline.

Drafting Your Three-Year Household Goals

1. The Top Five: Where does your home lack order? How do these areas affect your family? Maybe it's a cluttered kitchen counter that seems to be a magnet for junk mail, water bottles, school papers, and more. Maybe it's a hallway that looks like a small tornado hit a shoe store stockroom. Make the first step to creating order by owning and calling out the chaos. Name them! Call them out!

_____ affects our family by _____

_____.

_____ affects our family by _____

_____.

_____ affects our family by _____

_____.

_____ affects our family by _____

_____.

_____ affects our family by _____

_____.

Discuss these issues with your family and select three of them to focus on. Use a (*) to indicate the three that you chose.

2. The Solutions: Write practical solutions for these named problems, focusing on ideas that can be implemented immediately. For the cluttered kitchen counter example, practical solutions could be creating a file for mail, designating another area for water bottles, getting folders for school papers, and communicating this new organization system to other family members.

PROBLEM	SOLUTION
1.	
2.	
3.	

3. Craft Your Goals: Consider how you can turn these solutions into achievable goals for your family. For example, clear the kitchen counter nightly starting next month. Fine-tune your solutions, and you're ready to write your final draft!

Household Goal 1: _____

_____.

Household Goal 2: _____

_____.

Household Goal 3: _____

_____.

Now you can transfer these household goals to The Family Master Plan™.

CONCLUSION

Congratulations! Your Family Master Plan is complete.

And now that you have done the work, it's important to value it. I suggest you make your Family Master Plan look as nice as possible (print it out in full color, type it up, or get the person with the best penmanship in the family to write it) and hang it in a prominent place in your home. This will serve as a constant unspoken reminder that your family has not only a vision for its future but also a plan to get there. And even though they might not realize it, every time a family member passes by the document, it serves as a physical representation of how much they are loved, respected, and valued.

But keep in mind, the vision to see and plan something is just the first part of the process.

> "Vision without action is merely a dream.
> Action without vision just passes the time.
> Vision with action can change the world."
>
> *–Joel A. Barker*

PART-2

UNITY

Vision

Unity

Metrics

WELL-ORDERED FAMILY

Systems

Relationships

Discernment

™

"Building a visionary company is 1 percent vision and 99 percent perfect alignment. When you have a superb alignment, a visitor could drop in from outer space and infer your vision from the operations and activities of the company without ever reading it on paper or meeting a single senior executive."[11]

–JAMES C. COLLINS & JERRY I. PORRAS

11 James C. Collins and Jerry I. Porras, "Building Your Company's Vision," *Harvard Business Review* (2011).

CHAPTER

3

SUSTAINED UNITY

I just love this quote. I know the struggle involved with getting a group of employees working efficiently and effectively to achieve one unified vision. And I've seen it not just as a CEO myself but in other businesses I've been a consultant for and on boards for which I've served. In fact, I would say the only thing harder than devising a crystal clear vision is getting sustained unity around that vision.

Notice I say *sustained* unity. It's easy for everyone to get excited about a vision for a short time. It's easy to get lip service from employees who are more-or-less indifferent to the vision you hold so dear. Getting everyone to work toward that vision over an extended period, intentionally and actively, is extremely hard. If there was ever a secret sauce of success, this is it.

Family life is no different. If you can form and foster a visionary family, you will be a very rare family for sure. Yet there's absolutely nothing stopping you from doing this. The only thing in your way is the difficulty in focusing on your vision in a sustained fashion. Which is a bit like saying that the only thing in the way of your flying to the Moon is gravity.

Yet man has visited the Moon. And families have united around a common vision. Here are the best ways I know of to help your family stay on track through the thick and thin of daily life.

When you look through history at the most successful institutions, you quickly see that sustained unity of vision was a hallmark of their success.

THE APOSTLES OF JESUS CHRIST

Consider the rather simple and uneducated fishermen chosen by Christ to spread the Gospel throughout the world. They went to the ends of the earth: Paul to Rome, Thomas to India, James to Spain, Phillip to Ethiopia. And yet, they remained united for several key reasons.

- **Commissioned by Jesus:** Personally chosen and commissioned by Jesus, the apostles were entrusted with spreading His teachings and the Gospel worldwide.
- **Unity in Beliefs:** Despite diverse backgrounds, the apostles shared a strong belief in Jesus as the Son of God, unifying them in faith and purpose.
- **Sharing the Gospel:** Committed to spreading salvation through Christ, the apostles preached, established Christian communities, and shared the message of hope.
- **Council of Jerusalem:** In this significant gathering, the apostles resolved doctrinal and organizational matters, demonstrating unity, collaboration, and love.
- **Epistles and Letters:** The apostles wrote letters to guide and strengthen believers, fostering a shared vision and unity within the early Christian communities.
- **Martyrdom and Perseverance:** Facing persecution and martyrdom, the apostles' unwavering commitment to their shared vision inspired one another.
- **Successorship and Discipleship:** The appointment of successors and training of disciples ensured the continuity and expansion of the early Church's shared vision.

These factors, among others, contributed to the apostles' remarkable unity, making them an extraordinary example in history.

THE FOUNDING FATHERS

The Founding Fathers of the United States of America built a truly remarkable country. Their story is well-documented and serves as one of the greatest examples of radical unity. Consider the following contributing factors to their successful unity amidst their obvious differences.

- **Common Goal:** The Founding Fathers aimed to create a nation based on liberty, self-governance, and individual rights.
- **Declaration of Independence:** The 1776 declaration marked their shared vision to break away from British rule and establish an independent nation.
- **Constitutional Convention:** At the 1787 Convention, they drafted a balanced Constitution to protect rights and establish the rule of law.
- **Federalist Papers:** Key founders penned essays advocating a strong central government and protecting individual liberties.
- **Bill of Rights:** The first ten amendments ensured freedoms like speech, religion, and the right to a fair trial.
- **Peaceful Transition of Power:** They emphasized free elections and a smooth transfer of authority.

THE BOSTON CELTICS

I find it particularly interesting when radical unity prevails in competition. It is hard to argue with a win/loss record.

During the late 1950s to the late 1960s, the Boston Celtics dominated professional basketball. Legendary coach Red Auerbach and a roster of talented players, including Bill Russell, Bob Cousy, and John Havlicek, turned the Celtics into an NBA dynasty. They secured a total of eleven championships in thirteen seasons, including a record-setting eight consecutive titles from 1959 to 1966. This unprecedented achievement cemented their status as one of the greatest teams in sports history and set the championship ceiling higher than most imagined possible. The Celtics' success during this era is widely regarded as a testament to their exceptional teamwork, defensive prowess, and strategic coaching. In other words, they experienced radical unity as few others have.

FAMILY UNITY WON'T JUST HAPPEN

The previous examples show that unity around vision doesn't just happen. It must be managed. The apostles spent years preparing to go out. Even then, they had to reconvene for councils to keep their vision in order. The Founding Fathers had to continually work through their vision, just as the Continental Congress and Constitutional Conventions show. They had to duke it out with the Federalist Papers to keep working through the issues that were not resolved. The Celtics lost a total of 358 games in the era when they were considered one of the most dominant teams of all time. They didn't allow one loss to keep them from winning the next game.

How can we manage this sort of unity in our family? One things is certain: you can't wish it into being by force of personal will.

As always, the answer lies in systematic excellence.

CHAPTER

4

FAMILY MEETINGS

Call me old-fashioned, but I'm a fan of meetings. While the internet and working from home redesigned meetings, some businesses have a policy completely forbidding them at least one day of the week, and some research suggests fifty percent of the time spent in them is a total waste, I'm here to tell you that meetings are important. They are crucial for an organization's effective communication, collaboration, and issue resolution.

And a family is no different.

Wires get crossed. This is particularly true when you have teenagers. The teenage brain mass is perhaps the worst conduit for accurate communication on planet Earth. It is a like a huge game of "telephone" in which whatever emerges will be the opposite of what went in.

A teenager can ask Mom, "Can I go to out tonight with my friends?" And her answer of "No" will be twisted, contorted, coiled, curled, tangled, knotted, warped, bent, twirled, or construed as "Mom says I can go out with my friends tonight if it's okay with you."

While I'm exaggerating, I'm not overstating all that much. The eyes see and the ears hear what the brain *wishes* to see and hear. Family meetings, however informal, are a great way to get on the same page.

Remember, both a business and a family are groups of people working toward a common goal. Meetings allow your family to stay focused, track goals, and address issues in a timely manner. They allow you to work *on* the family rather than solely working *in* the family.

Your family meetings are your greatest tool for forging sustained unity. They can help desensitize certain topics over time. Regularly discussing difficult subjects, such as poor habits or behaviors, creates an open and comfortable environment for addressing them. It avoids making individuals defensive and allows for constructive conversations and growth within the family.

I have seen in numerous organizations--particularly in religious and non-profit organizations—how the sin of hubris settles in the heart of old-school executives who conclude they no longer need regular meetings, agendas for meetings, or concrete action items to conclude a meeting. The typical old dog feels he has so much experience that routine, preparation, and follow through are for other people; his own wisdom and charisma will carry the day. Hubris. That's all there is to it.

Remember that hubris for the ancient Greeks was when the hero, who had many god-given talents and abilities, became prideful in these gifts and overshot, reached too far, overstepped in such a way as to offend the gods.

In business, great success often leads to a complacency of "I got this" or a "we didn't use these fancy agendas in my heyday. Why the hell would I use them now?"

Well, times have changed, my old friend. Meetings these days are meant to have a point, to be concise, to be for collaboration, for specific action items and measuring outcomes. The boss man bloviating at the head of the table, with everyone nodding and kissing butt, is done.

Meetings are no longer monologues. They are dialogues. If you want to give a monologue, then give an address at a podium, but don't pretend it is a meeting if you aren't actually gathering for two-way communication.

The same is true in family life. Families become a little prideful in their opinion of themselves. Spouses think they know each other well enough to skip the basics of sound communication. Parents often think they invest so much time with their kids that the last thing they need to do is have an organized meeting with them. If asked, most families would say they know exactly what they want out of life, and yet, when asked to articulate it, you get gobbledygook or half-baked ideas.

Family meetings help keep the vision clear, the communication open, and the negative emotions at bay. The *Well-Ordered Family*™ has four different types of meetings.

- The Weekly Marriage Check-In™
- The Weekly Family Huddle™
- The Quarterly Family Meeting™
- The Annual Family Council™

To get a complete understanding of how each one contributes to forming sustained unity around your Family Master Plan, let's take a closer look at each type of meeting. We'll start with the shorter and simpler ones and work our way up.

THE WEEKLY MARRIAGE CHECK-IN™

The Weekly Marriage Check-In™ is a very different meeting than the others. In fact, you could argue it's more of a heart-to-heart than a meeting. Ideally, it is spiritually intimate. Here, you have a chance to bare your soul a little. If you can talk about the movements of the heart that lie beneath the logistics of the week, please do so.
The purpose isn't to cover the lengthy to-do list (though that often arises). The point of this check-in is to take the spiritual and emotional temperature of your spouse so that you can be an even better soulmate over the next seven days. You might already do this informally to some degree or another. It is time to make it explicit, consistent, and intentional. On the next page you will find a sample agenda.

THE WEEKLY MARRIAGE CHECK-IN™	
SEGUE AND PRAYER	1 MIN
LAST WEEK'S WINS	2 MINS
NEXT WEEK'S HOPES	2 MINS
POTENTIAL STRESSORS	2 MINS
PLEASE HELP	2 MINS
RECAP AND PRAYER	1 MIN

Segue and Prayer (1 min)

Get settled and start with a short prayer if you are comfortable doing so.

Last Week's Wins (2 mins)

It's important to take the time to share with each other the wins over the last week or so. It communicates you care, enables you to celebrate as a couple, and sets a positive and affirming tone.

Obviously, you can share things that "got done" on the to-do list. That's great. But remember, this is the one scheduled time each week to go a little deeper. Seize the moment.

Be sure to give verbal and visual approval of your spouse's wins. From experience, it's difficult at times for me to see my wife's wins as wins. And vice versa. Why? Because we're so opposite of each other. Things she feels really good about, like getting the playroom carpets cleaned, I struggle to pay attention to. (Don't get me wrong; I'm glad she cares. Ugly carpets just don't bother me.) This could be a great victory for her because she feels that some semblance of order returned to the upstairs of our house. Likewise, my little victories at work can seem very remote and impractical to her. But they are important to me, nonetheless.

Next Week's Hopes (2 mins)

It is important to note that this is not a scorecard. It doesn't have to be a S.M.A.R.T. goal—something quantifiable, like the many other goals discussed in this book. These are hopes of the heart that each of you have. A hope could certainly be a quantifiable goal, like "get the garage organized." But I hope (no pun intended) that these are *qualitative* in nature.

Here are some examples:

- I hope there is less arguing between the kids.
- I hope the mini conflict with my friend dissipates.
- I hope the kids don't pick up the stomach bug from their friends.
- I hope it doesn't rain during the little guy's birthday party. (Better include this in your closing prayer, as well.)

When you say "I hope," it provides a window into your soul. We all know you can't control whether it rains during the birthday party. But showing your spouse you long for the little guy to have a great time outdoors with his friends has value. Spouses need to know what's in each other's heart. It is effective. It is beautiful.

Potential Stressors (2 mins)

After each of you has opened his or her heart, it is a perfect opportunity to acknowledge upcoming challenges. A lot of stress comes from the unknown. Verbalizing helps take some of that anxiety away. It also lets your spouse know you will be taking on these challenges together.

Here are some examples:

- Credit card bill is due on Tuesday and an unforeseen car repair needs to be made
- Johnny has a test in a particularly challenging subject on Wednesday
- Aunt Martha is scheduled for surgery Friday

Please Help (2 mins)

Now that you've acknowledged the potential stressors, it's a great time to simply ask for help. This shouldn't be a logistics conversation. We'll get to that later.

This is the perfect time to ask your spouse for help in a particular way or a specific area. *Warning!* Be sure *not* to turn this into a "Please help me by giving up all your bad habits."

Consider examples like this:

- Wife asks husband, "Please help me with the conflict between the fourteen-year-old and the twelve-year-old. It's really wearing on me."
- Husband asks wife, "Please help me find a way to spend time with the teenagers. I feel too distant from them."
- Wife asks husband, "Please help me get organized so I can start working out again. I feel so run down."
- Husband asks wife, "Please help me detach from late night TV. I gotta get back to reading."

These are just a few examples to show how spouses can ask for help to be a better person and bring more peace and joy into the family. Remember, it isn't logistical. It's spiritual.

Recap and Prayer (1 min)

Recap the most important points raised and sign off with a little prayer together. The goal is for spouses to feel heard, be on the same page, and face the coming week with a renewed spirit of commitment and unity.

THE WEEKLY FAMILY HUDDLE™

The Weekly Family Huddle is an opportunity to touch base with your family on the logistics issues, opportunities, and threats for the upcoming week. I call this a huddle to keep the focus short and to the point. Some businesses have "morning huddles" or "standup meetings" to emphasize how quick everything should move.

A football team goes into a huddle to call the next play. They aren't hashing things out. They aren't arguing. There might be a verbal pat on the back or quick word of motivation, but 80 percent of the huddle is calling the play. Your family huddle should emulate this. It is only ten minutes. What on earth can you accomplish in ten minutes? A lot, especially when you avoid the tangents. Here is the sample agenda:

THE WEEKLY FAMILY HUDDLE™	
SEGUE AND PRAYER	1 MIN
WEEK PREVIEW	6 MINS
OPPORTUNITIES	1 MIN
THREATS	1 MIN
RECAP AND PRAYER	1 MIN

Segue and Prayer (1 min)

Here, there is very little time to chat. Just call everyone into the huddle. You might even holler, "Huddle up everyone!" Consider the dining room table or the kitchen counter as places to meet. It should be right in the middle of your Grand Central Station.

You have a full sixty seconds to get people focused. Turn off the TV, hand a sippy cup to the toddler to keep her quiet, corral the slow-moving teenager down the stairs—whatever you need to do to get things moving.

But try to begin with prayer. Keep it short. "Lord, keep us united this week. All that we do, we do for Your glory. Amen." That takes me about eight seconds to pray. Come up with your own. Do the same one each week, or something different each week. But short and sweet is the main point.

Week Preview (6 mins)

Most times you gather with your family, you want everyone to put away their phones. Not here. I usually start with, "Get your phones out and open your calendars." After all, this is a logistics meeting as much as anything. A football huddle makes sure players are running and blocking in the right places so the play will work. The family huddle makes sure parents and kids are in the right places so the week will work.

I recommend going day by day. Start with Monday (assuming your Weekly Family Huddle is on Sunday night). Go through each day of the week to get on the same page. Use the spaces provided on The Weekly Family Huddle™ Agenda to jot down notes, conflicts, or issues that can't be resolved here and now.

Here's an example.

- **Monday**
  - No issues. Just same practice schedule as usual for the teenager.
- **Tuesday**
  - Mom says little kids have a doctor's appointment at 9:00 a.m., but she really doesn't want to take the baby. She asks if Dad can stay home/work from home Tuesday morning.

* **Wednesday**
  - Dad has a business colleague in town all day Wednesday. Availability to text and talk on the phone will be limited. Also has business dinner Wednesday night with the colleague. This means he can't drive little kids to coach-pitch.
  - Teenager had a plan to hang out with friends on Wednesday night after practice. Really doesn't want to babysit that night.
  - Mom has a meeting at church on Wednesday night. She can drop off kids at coach-pitch, but she can't pick them up. Plus, she needs the teenager to babysit until she gets home. She says she will get another parent to bring the little kids home from practice. But she says the teenager has to be home by 6:30 p.m. so she can get to her church meeting. Teenager grumbles but gets over it.

* **Thursday**
  - No issues. No practices. Whew.
  - Dad asks if they can plan on eating as a family. Mom asks if he will pick up stuff on the way home from work for a cookout.
  - Dad tells teenager to be home for dinner by 6:00 p.m.
  - Teenager says his friend was supposed to be coming over to play some basketball.
  - Dad says invite the friend to stay for dinner. (It's not perfect for Dad, but it is no big deal either.)

* **Friday**
  - Teenager game in the evening.
  - Dad says he wants to go. Mom says she hasn't seen a game yet this season. Dad agrees to stay with the baby so Mom can enjoy the game.

* **Saturday**
  - Mom says little kids have coach-pitch game. Dad wonders why this wasn't on his calendar. Mom explains the schedule changed, so everything in his calendar is wrong. Dad asks for Mom to send new schedule right then and there. She does so. Dad makes a mental note to update calendar.
  - Dad says his goal was to clean out the garage on Saturday. They plan on it happening in the afternoon after the game.

- **Sunday**
  - Mom suggests keeping the Sabbath holy by having a great family day. This begins with going to early Church service, followed by family brunch and watching football together.
  - Teenager asks if friends can come over to watch football game. Dad makes a note to invite adult kids and spouses over for the football game and an early dinner.

Opportunities (1 min)

If there is time, it is worth the leader of the meeting asking the simple question: What are the opportunities for the family this week? This can be an opportunity for family time, a victory in the classroom, in sports, or at work.

Other opportunities might include:

- A productive meeting with the work colleague coming in town
- Enjoying a family dinner
- To plan a great family day on Sunday

Threats (1 min)

Threats are those people, activities, or logistics that are likely to disturb the peace and joy of the family. "Okay guys," the family leader might say, "what are the threats this week?"

Threats might include:

- A busy Wednesday that's likely to cause transportation conflicts
- Too much TV in the evenings, given that the family has been trying to cut back on screen time
- Saturday chores spilling over into Sunday

The point here is for family members to mention those things that come to mind and get them written down. No discussion is needed. You only have sixty seconds anyway. More time here is unproductive. If an issue does merit more conversation, talk about it offline.

Recap and Prayer (1 min)

As always, recap the most important one or two points and quickly say a prayer to conclude the meeting. Break!

And it's back to the game of life.

THE QUARTERLY FAMILY MEETING™

Now that we're addressing family spiritual and logis-
tics issues weekly, it's time to go a little more in-depth
with The Quarterly Family Meeting™ that focuses on
the procedural. But don't worry. If you think your
family doesn't have time to waste on anything that
borders on the theoretical or impractical, you can guarantee mine doesn't! The
Quarterly Family Meeting™ is designed to happen once every three months
and last for thirty minutes. The goal here is to keep track of the most important issues that affect the family on more than just a day-in and day-out basis.

At first glance, you may be thinking there isn't enough time to discuss the
issues. You're right! It's purposely designed that way. Let's take a closer look
at each section.

THE QUARTERLY FAMILY MEETING™	
SEGUE AND PRAYER	2 MINS
LAST QUARTER'S MAJOR WINS	5 MINS
REVIEW LAST QUARTER'S FAMILY ROCKS	5 MINS
CHOOSE NEXT QUARTER'S FAMILY ROCKS	10 MINS
REVIEW OF THE FAMILY SCORECARD™	5 MINS
RECAP AND PRAYER	3 MINS

Segue and Prayer (2 mins)

Take time to get everyone situated, eliminate last minute distractions, get the small talk out of the way, and begin with prayer.

Last Quarter's Major Wins (5 mins)

Allow each person to share last quarter's "wins." This can include improvements they made, grades, sports, friendships, habits formed, or simply events they enjoyed.

Usually, it is wise to stick to an agenda. Here, however, if the Spirit so moves you, allow this to linger beyond the time allotted. If your family is speaking about victories, improvements, and fun times, by all means, let it keep going. Some disagree with this. From my experience, the opportunity for busy families to revel in positivity is so rare that I think you should seize the moment when God gives it to you.

Review Last Quarter's Family Rocks (5 mins)

For the moment let's just take "rocks" to mean "three-month goals." We will dive much deeper into the concept—and explain why I call them "rocks"—in chapter 10.

Review your Family Rocks in rapid style. Try to allow for just a one or two sentence explanation of why the rock was hit or missed.

Only five minutes to review last quarter's Family Rocks? The reason the time for review is so short is that it's not a time to talk about the issues. If you want to discuss in depth why a particular rock was not hit, talk about it "offline." The reason is simple. As soon as you dive into these subjects, all sorts of dynamics present themselves. Emotions become frayed, other issues can arise, the other people in the meeting check out. By getting updated on a hit or miss, you see what needs to be discussed in depth but keep the meeting going.

IMPORTANT The commitment to keep the meeting moving keeps everyone engaged and drastically improves each participant's willingness to attend and contribute next time.

Choose Next Quarter's Family Rocks (10 mins)

Discuss three to five Family Rocks for the upcoming ninety days. Err on the side of less. No one remembers numerous priorities. Aim for S.M.A.R.T. rocks so everyone knows if it is hit or not.

Here are a few examples of rocks that are *not* recommended:

- **Be nice:** How can this be measured?
- **Having joy in the home:** As laudable as this is, can you measure it? Maybe. If so, articulate. But "joy" itself is not specific, easily measured, or time-bound.
- **Exercise more virtue:** Again, as stated, you will have no idea if this was hit or missed. You might have a "feel" for whether things have improved, but arguments will certainly ensue if you just say to someone "you are less virtuous than before." If they said, "Prove it!" how would you do so? If you can tie virtue to metrics (which I think you can), then you can make your case in a more convincing, charitable, and respectful way.

Be sure to pick quarterly rocks that you can nail down. The family needs clarity and objectivity. Assign a specific family member as the person responsible for making sure that a rock gets done. A good place to keep track of your Family Rocks is on The Family Scorecard™.

Review of The Family Scorecard™ (5 mins)

Rapidly review your Family Scorecard. We'll discuss this important tool in chapter 12. It is important that the scorecard gets filled out prior to this meeting. Ideally, your scorecard is updated weekly. Perhaps it's displayed on the refrigerator or another prominent place in your home.

In this meeting, don't dwell on the numbers. Just "keep the score." If you want to discuss something on the scorecard, schedule the meeting right then and there. Maybe it is immediately following this meeting, maybe not. But keep the meeting flow going.

For example, let's say on your Family Scorecard that your fourteen-year-old's screen time was twice what you wanted it to be. Perhaps there is a one-line explanation of "Remember, Mom, you gave me permission to watch that movie on my phone?" Okay. Fine. Valid explanation. But if the time was spent texting and using social media, now we have a disciplinary issue.

It is recommended that these family meetings *not* be used for discipline. Get on the same page about goals, performance, and issues (including discipline) that need to be discussed separately. In these situations, I've found saying something like, "We will talk about this tomorrow morning before school," to be effective. This way, everyone knows the teenager isn't getting away with something. And by naming the issue and the time and place it will be discussed, there is no ambiguity. The beauty of this is clearly calling out and spotlighting the issue without derailing the meeting.

If you're a parent struggling with the idea of not using the meeting for discipline, think about it this way. Imagine a boss that uses meetings to ramrod his employees in public. It not only embarrasses the person but also derails the meeting at hand. It's far more effective for the boss to say, "This is a serious issue that needs to be discussed. Are you available tomorrow at 9:00 a.m. to talk about it?" A simple statement like this is deceptively powerful. "Oh crap! The boss is taking this seriously," is the thought that goes through everyone's mind. And yet, the supervisor earns respect for not going off on the tangent. It also communicates that the boss is in control of his own thoughts and emotions and values everyone's time. This translates to confidence in leadership.

Parenting is not all that different. Control these meetings with confidence and intentionality. You will get way more mileage out of these meetings by knowing what they are for and, just as importantly, what they are not for.

Recap and Prayer (3 mins)

Bring the meeting to a close by thanking everyone, recapping any highlights, and restating the quarter's rocks (three-month goals). Make sure you keep a copy of the Quarterly Family Meeting™ Agenda for reference at next quarter's meeting. Finish with a prayer.

THE ANNUAL FAMILY COUNCIL™

Business often speaks of "strategic planning," but this is not very applicable for families. The term "family council" is more fitting. You get to choose who is in your family council. Maybe in the early years, it is just the spouses. Or perhaps you choose to include an outsider to join your Annual Family Council. This could be a trusted friend, an aunt or uncle, or even a parent/grandparent, particularly if they live with you. The latter idea should be used with extreme caution, as intergenerational family dynamics can be tricky waters to navigate.

As your kids get older, they can join your Annual Family Council™ and actually contribute! In my experience, by the age of seven or eight, kids can start to follow an adult conversation and contribute in their own way. You will see an immediate payoff by incorporating their comments.

Teenagers, as we all know, are much trickier. They can make or break the entire experience. Often, they bring a sour attitude to the event. Slouching body language, eyes glued to the phone, and curt answers to the questions posed can, frankly, ruin the whole thing. On the other hand, an engaged teenager can energize the entire family and bring great joy to Mom and Dad.

Experience shows certain tips work for getting the best out of your teenager in The Annual Family Council™ (or any family meeting for that matter). On the next page you will find a list of tips for engaging your teenager in family meetings.

TIPS FOR ENGAGING YOUR TEENAGER IN FAMILY MEETINGS

1. Give them a big heads up: Tell them well in advance about the meeting so they aren't surprised. They need emotional time to adjust to the idea.

2. Ask them to prepare: Asking teenagers to bring their own ideas to the table means the world to them, even if they don't immediately perceive it. This could include areas of improvement they see or concerns they have. Perhaps you could ask them to research a particular issue in discussion. But be clear: this is not a venue to complain about anything and everything. It is a time to maturely discuss how the family can improve.

3. Treat them like an adult: Remember that the whole reason for teenage attitude is because they are stuck between the status of kid and adult. It might be helpful to assign them as the scribe of the meeting. Ask their opinion about how to handle the little kid issues. Ask about their experience as a little kid in this family, and how could Mom and Dad improve the experience for the next kid. You might find the teenager dissociates a little on The Vision+ Statement because it is a remote concept and a bit obscure. But you will likely find that the teenager has a lot to say about the Core Virtues you choose. The Core Virtues hit home for them. And they have something to say about them. It's a topic you can engage with them each quarter. Ask their opinion on how each Core Virtue is being lived out in the family. If you listen, you will find some insight that you did not expect.

4. Pray for your teenager prior to the meeting: Here, you should pray for (a) your mature and engaged teenager to show up rather than the immature and checked out teenager, and (b) your own patience with the teenager during the meeting. Just go ahead and prepare yourself for potential disagreement. If you handle this well, the rewards are immeasurable.

Let's look at a potential agenda for The Annual Family Council™:

THE ANNUAL FAMILY COUNCIL™	
SEGUE AND PRAYER	5 MINS
LAST YEAR'S MAJOR WINS	10 MINS
LAST YEAR'S CHALLENGES	5 MINS
REVIEW OF THE FAMILY MASTER PLAN™	15 MINS
REVIEW OF THE FAMILY SCORECARD™	20 MINS
RECAP AND PRAYER	5 MINS

Segue and Prayer (5 mins)

Take time to get everyone situated, eliminate last-minute distractions, get the small talk out of the way, and begin with prayer. Five minutes is allotted because no one in the real world sits down exactly on time and starts working immediately. There is always a buffer.

I recommend you begin with prayer, even if you're uncomfortable doing so. Perhaps you pray extemporaneously. Perhaps you simply say the Lord's Prayer. Prayer clearly shows the event has begun and that it is a serious endeavor.

Last Year's Major Wins (10 mins)

Again, it's extremely important to begin on a positive note. In fact, I have learned how powerful it is to begin virtually every meeting at work with a quick list of recent wins, personal or professional. It immediately sets the tone. I'm indebted to *Strategic Coach* for helping me form this habit. Every time I receive coaching virtually or in-person, my coach always begins this way. In fact, the coaches send out an email the day before our scheduled call and remind us to reflect on our recent wins. *Strategic Coach* even has an app now called *WinStreak* in which you simply jot down the wins of each day. As easy as it sounds, it keeps the mind positive and focused on how to build on these wins.

This is precisely why a full ten minutes is allotted for last year's major wins. This can include improvements made, grades, sports, friendships, habits formed, or simply events the family enjoyed. It's totally okay if you exceed the ten-minute time limit here. This helps to set a strong positive tone for the entire meeting.

Last Year's Challenges (5 mins)

It might seem odd to follow the major wins with last year's challenges. The truth is that you have to cover these in one way or another at some point in your family meeting cadence. Notice only five minutes is allotted. It is half the time of the wins.

Here, it is recommended to do a rapid-fire roundtable on the challenges endured. It is important not to linger. Do not allow this to turn into arguments or insults. Make sure it stays empathetic and to the point.

There are two likely possibilities if a discussion on challenges lingers: first, it becomes a complaining session about people and events. Try to move beyond this quickly. But second, it can become a very therapeutic opportunity for someone suffering in your family to speak up. As the leader of this family meeting, it is important for you to be prayerfully attuned to these dynamics. If you are Christian, ask the Holy Spirit for the gift of wisdom and counsel. If the discussion is needed at that time, if the family is rallying behind each other, if healing is in process, by all means, forget the agenda.

Your family is very clearly not a business. You aren't working toward just efficiency or productivity. Even in business, issues come up in meetings and you have to throw the agenda out of the window. Why? Because we work with human beings! They have their own thoughts and emotions, joys and sorrows. Any business leader who forgets this isn't worth his salt.

Multiply this times nearly infinity when it comes to your family. So even though I provide you with the agenda, I'm the first one to say, "forget the agenda" when the Spirit moves you to do so.

With that said, once the challenges have been covered in quick order, we move on to reviewing The Family Master Plan™.

Review of The Family Master Plan™ (15 mins)

If you've completed it, read through your Family Master Plan line by line. See if anything major has changed. The point isn't to rewrite it but to simply remind each other of its contents and ask if anything significant should be amended.

Here is a great time to choose a new patron for the year. If this conversation will take longer than you have available, why not schedule a dinner in the next week to eat together and discuss the patron for the coming year? The point is to not get overly bogged down on any one issue. Schedule a time to handle it and move on.

If you haven't done The Family Master Plan™, there's no need for concern. Just use this time to roughly discuss your family vision and perhaps brainstorm on some core virtues.

Review of The Family Scorecard™ (20 mins)

Every Annual Family Council is an opportunity to review the scorecard and make it better for the following year.

Where did your family excel? Where did it struggle? What scorecard items were most effective to keep tabs on? What categories should you eliminate for next year? What should you add? What surprised you? Did your family meet your expectations? How can you do better?

This conversation is allotted the most time in this meeting to make sure all council members have a chance to weigh in with their opinions and feel heard. Keep in mind, this is not a license to criticize or complain about other family members. It is the time to assess your yearly progress, discuss the pros and cons of how you measured and tracked that progress, and brainstorm new ways to improve this process moving forward.

Recap and Prayer (5 mins)

Bring the meeting to a close by thanking everyone, recapping any highlights, and restating the priorities for the new year. Finish with a prayer.

THE FAMILY MEETING CADENCE

The cadence part of Family Meeting Cadence refers to the annual schedule of different types of meetings. Now that we've gone over the four different types of meetings, you probably have a good idea of how the Family Meeting Cadence looks over an extended period of time.

- **The Annual Family Council**™ (1 hour)—Strategic
  - Recap previous year
  - Deep review of The Family Master Plan™
  - Deep review The Family Scorecard™

- **The Quarterly Family Meeting**™ (30 minutes)—Procedural
  - Recap previous quarter
  - Review Family Rocks/Choose new Rocks
  - Quick review The Family Scorecard™

- **The Weekly Family Huddle**™ (10 minutes)—Logistical
  - Preview upcoming week
  - Coordinate schedules
  - Set further discussions if necessary

- **The Weekly Marriage Check-In**™ (10 minutes)—Spiritual
  - · Connect and celebrate last week's wins
  - · Share next week's hopes
  - · Ask spouse for help

This looks like a lot. And it will feel like a lot *if* you haven't worked out the family vision and made unity a high priority. But when vision is clear and family unity is valued, these meetings can fly by and leave you looking forward to the progress you'll make at the next one.

THE FAMILY MEETING CADENCE MASTER LIST™

Now that you understand the value of these regular meetings, the next step is making them happen. The Well-Ordered Family™ is about real families, not theoretical ones. So, it's wildly important that we don't just talk about having these meetings but actually make them happen. Consistently.

Just yesterday (I kid you not), my wife mentioned that we needed another family meeting to review the standards for cleaning, particularly for the upstairs. The kids have been mastering the art of deception and pushing clutter to the far corners of the playroom, or throwing all the toys in one big bucket rather than sorting them correctly.

I explained that, yes, certainly, we could call a meeting and make a more thorough list of requirements for each chore. But I also reminded her that we had our Annual Family Council on January 2nd, and it was now only February 18th. We might want to hold off and have a thorough Quarterly Family Meeting at the end of this quarter, the end of March.

We didn't make a decision then and there. But you can see the value of saying, "Okay. This is important to you. Yes. I agree. But if we follow our cadence, then your concern will be addressed soon enough."

Of course, we might end up having this meeting the next weekend. What matters is having a process that you can rely on that collects concerns, and reliably addresses them at a set time.

Year: _____

THE FAMILY MEETING CADENCE MASTER LIST™			
MEETING	**DATE(S)**	**STATUS**	**NOTES**
THE ANNUAL FAMILY COUNCIL™	_____	COMPLETE / NOT COMPLETE	
THE QUARTERLY FAMILY MEETING™	_____ _____ _____ _____	COMPLETE / NOT COMPLETE COMPLETE / NOT COMPLETE COMPLETE / NOT COMPLETE COMPLETE / NOT COMPLETE	
THE WEEKLY FAMILY HUDDLE™	EVERY _____	MISSED DATES:	
THE WEEKLY MARRIAGE CHECK-IN™	EVERY _____	MISSED DATES:	

(FYI—In this instance, I wanted to push the meeting to the end of March for a few reasons: 1. I like the cadence; 2. It isn't good to have meetings when the nerves are frayed; and 3. I should try to prep the kids and my tools for the best meeting possible so that Ashley appreciates the effort and is satisfied by the outcome.)

In order to provide visual reminders that a Family Meeting Cadence is important for keeping unity, The Family Meeting Cadence Master List ™ was created. This document doesn't warrant pride of place, like The Master Family Plan ™ or The Family Scorecard Generator™. But perhaps there is a spot in the house, like Mom or Dad's desk, or a wall in the pantry or mudroom. This way the master list is seen on occasion and reminds everyone to schedule the meetings and put the meeting dates and times on their own calendars. As you can see, The Family Meeting Cadence Master List ™ must be updated regularly. Using a pencil with an eraser can allow you to keep the same document on the wall rather than going through the cumbersome process of reprinting.[12]

CONCLUSION

If your family does not think there is a lot to talk about, then, frankly, you are in deep trouble. It reminds me of the person who, on a whim, examines his conscience and finds very little to confess and repent of. In fact, he's pleased as punch with himself! The angels in heaven might learn a lesson or two just by watching him.

In my opinion, this person is like one who has lost his vision to such an extent that he no longer remembers the light. On the other hand, one who examines his conscience daily finds many imperfections and sees the greater possibilities; he comes to understand sins of commission and sins of omission.

The more your family meets, the more there will be to discuss. If you continually discuss your long-term vision, review your systems for improvement,

---

12 This simple point goes to the heart of Lean Six Sigma's notion of waste. The "rework" and "motion" and "waiting" of printing something is often avoidable. In fact, how many times has your printer been out of ink or out of paper? In this event, the chances of you actually typing in the new data points in the document and reprinting have dropped dramatically. Thus, whenever you can use edited documents, you automatically eliminate numerous forms of waste.

discuss the smoothness of day-to-day logistics, and even touch on the emotions whirling around in the hearts of each other, you will begin to see countless ways to improve without necessarily feeling huge amounts of guilt. You will simply and maturely assess your current state, recognize your imperfections as a family, and seek to steadily improve.

This will provide your family with the unity necessary to help realize its vision. And now it's time to build on that vision and unity by implementing the systems your family needs to thrive.

PART-3

SYSTEMS

Vision

Unity

Metrics

WELL-ORDERED FAMILY

Systems

Relationships

Discernment

TM

"Every system is perfectly designed
to get the results it gets."

–W. EDWARDS DEMING

6

SYSTEMATIC
EXCELLENCE

Here is a typical day in the Gallagher family. Ashley usually gets up with a baby at night (whether this is a nursing baby or just a little guy wandering downstairs). By nature Ashley is a morning person, but being pregnant or having a baby for significant portions of her life tends to change that routine. She may have gotten up hours before me and be just getting back to bed.

I wake up before the little guys do and let Ashley sleep as much as possible. At this time, I try to say my prayers, plan my day in my planner, and drink large quantities of coffee. At different points in my life I have "attacked the morning" as a card-carrying member of the five a.m. club, but recently I keep it more low key. My ideal morning routine is prayer, spiritual writing, and coffee. The little kids come trickling downstairs around six or so. The lethargic toddlers are the best at this time of day. They cuddle up on and around you. You give them a bottle or sippy-cup, and you are in parental paradise. I remind myself, "This will not last forever," and it doesn't.

Soon a few more trickle down, at least one of whom will have woken up on the wrong side of the bed.

My favorite part of the morning is sharing coffee with Ashley. We go through our day a little, but don't plan a campaign. You can't jump into logistics instantly, at least I can't. Homeschooling has allowed us to be perhaps a bit slower in the mornings than many families, which is a great blessing. But at times we have loaded up the kids to get to 7:00 A.M. Mass. Those mornings are really hard! At other times we have had kids in homeschool co-ops where they begin school days the way most other kids do—by traipsing to class at the crack of dawn.

Sometimes I have had the pleasure of taking the older kids to Mass before school. Those are special times.

We tend to measure our time by semesters, and each semester is different for us. Sometimes mornings are slow and soothing, sometimes fast and hectic.

I go to work (whether at my home office, which my seventeen-year-old son built me in the backyard, or at the business headquarters), and Ashley begins her day with homeschooling. She is a seasoned pro at this point, but that's only after years of concerted effort to learn what to teach and how to teach it. She usually sits at the kitchen table and works with the little guys while the more self-sufficient kids go to the home classroom or their bedrooms and crank out their own schoolwork independently.

The notion that homeschool kids lack "socialization" should be considered by this point beyond silly, at least for us. Nobody is missing out in that regard. My kids have so many social events that it is hard to keep it all straight. My wife has worked hard to ensure proper friendships, fun activities, and homeschool activities with other families. I myself struggle daily to maintain a basic idea of who is where and what is going on.

Ashley does an amazing job keeping the trains running on time all day long. I'm a blessed man. Ashley handles the bills, the insurance companies, and anything else that could potentially involve paperwork or dealing with bureaucratic processes. My time is largely spent on running my business, spending time with the kids, and helping Ashley with whatever is needed around the house. The deep truth to our "well-ordered family" is that she is our secret weapon.

Things get interesting in the evening, when there are evening events, such as sports, which can become a scheduling job that rivals the travails of a major transportation company. And we have been through the cycle repeatedly at different times. At one point, we had five kids on baseball teams at once.[13] These days we make it a rule to hold off on sports teams until high school, which for us has significantly improved our homelife and family time. Currently, I have three boys on the same high school basketball team. It is a joy to watch them play together. But it is also a joy that two of the three can drive to practice during the week.

You can imagine our house at the end of the day. The dishes are piled a mile high. There is enough food on the floor to feed a small village. No matter what rules we set, a bowl of cereal inevitably finds its way upstairs. Even if we barricade the pantry with a barbed wire fence, somehow the four-year-old sneaks in and spills a bag of popcorn across the floor. And let's leave the bathrooms out of this picture. You simply don't want to know!

Yet it is a joyful house. But within those twelve hours of joy, these rug rats can do an incredible amount of damage.

And so, the chores begin. These days, it runs very smoothly, which is one of the main themes of this book, but in the past, chores were a battle. We'll talk about the power of a chore-chart shortly. For now, let me say that if you came in to my house at 6:30 in the evening you just might see a four-year-old vacuuming or sweeping (rather poorly, but steadily moving the handle). While you can't hold them to a high standard, you can expect the little guys to pitch in. Even a three-year-old loves to vacuum . . . and the twelve-year-old hates going back over the same area. But that is his chore. Such is life.

Training begins as young as possible. If I change my two-year-old's diaper, I try to get her to say thank you (yes, that's right) and I encourage her to throw the diaper away. She's two; she can do it! And of course she gets a round of applause if she manages to get close to the trash can. The point is that self-reliance begins as early as possible. Why? Because enabling

---

13 One time, we just couldn't get the kids to their different fields at the same time. We needed another driver. I told Ashley, "Just throw Aiden in an Uber." She looked at me in horror, given that Aiden was twelve-years old, not sure if I was serious. "You are out of your mind," she said. "That is way too dangerous." "You're right, honey," I replied. "That was stupid of me. Instead, give Aiden my handgun, then throw him in an Uber." I laughed at myself. She stared at me. With a moment to laugh and breathe, we then proceeded to solve the problem.

self-centeredness and laziness begins right away, as well. Don't fall into the trap of doing everything for your kids. And when you have fifteen, it simply isn't possible anyway.

After chores, or even toward the tail end of chores, we begin our family prayer.

At our house, we pray the Catholic Rosary. We let the youngest kids possible lead the prayers, a different kid for each decade of the Rosary. Admittedly, this is often too fast paced, and perhaps lacks the piety that one might expect. But there is also something beautiful about praying on the move and incorporating prayer into doing the dishes, or yelling prayers over the noise of the vacuum. Since confession is ongoing for us Catholics, I regularly confess lack of piety, particularly failing to lead my family in piety. And usually my Pastor tells me to go easy on myself. God can hear us over a garbage disposal's hum.

For whatever reason, I hate bath time. My wife does that.

I know, I know. The kids are adorable, splashing around in the tub, etc. I get it. You are right. But then there's kneeling on a hard tile floor, getting splashed, and washing kids who are squirming and playing. I hate it when the little one gets soap in her eyes and screams. I do it when necessary, but often remind my wife (and to no avail) that the kings of medieval England only bathed once a year.

So, my wife or older kids usually take on the momentous task of keeping us all clean. I focus my evening efforts on bedtime.

When I'm extremely tired or in a bad mood, I admittedly scoot the kids off to bed, tell them a pretty lame story or read Dr. Seuss at warp-speed.

Then it is prayer time, and I confess to rattling off a rather pathetic litany at such times. "God bless Mommy and Daddy, Aiden, Mary, Patrick . . . . Help us be kind, gentle, and loving. Please take care of the sick and the poor. Forgive us for our sins. Amen."

But when I'm at the top of my game, I come up with some great and even inspiring stories, or at least extremely elaborate tales. These are often part of an ongoing family series, now a tradition, called, "Uncle Ickybob and the Magical Encyclopedia Set."

In this saga, Uncle Ickybob reads a particular encyclopedia entry to Little Boy Jack. But Jack ends up inside the story somehow, and (we hope!) falls asleep there. When I'm on my game, night time prayers are more directed and discerning. I manage to pull intentions out of even the little kids, teaching them to verbalize their own spiritual life and longings.

In short, the bedtime routine can be marvelous when done well. And it can be aggravating and full of conflict when done poorly. Sometimes a three-year-old is going to fight you almost to the death at bedtime, and there is nothing you can do about it. At those times, all you can do is embrace the suffering and move on.

She's a kid. It just comes with the territory. The good times will make up for the bad times. That I can promise. I've been through this enough times to develop statistical models!

Sometimes after putting the little guys to bed, I have to edit papers for my older kids, including for the college kids. I try to take this burden off my wife, given that she taught them how to read to begin with. At times, I worry that I have failed to teach them the finer aspects of writing. Their typical mistakes drive me bonkers. I've found that I am a better teacher of other people's kids than my own. How foolish I can be when approaching my own. Usually I try to keep it cool and walk them through the basics of composing a paper. It is similar in its way to teaching someone how to drive. I do get frustrated so easily, but have learned to tamp that down by recalling, "Oh yeah, they haven't done this before. I have."

Parenthood essentially never is done. So evenings often end with helping the big kids with their big kid stuff as they phase into the even more daunting adult stuff we all must face.

Too often, I find myself staying up late waiting for the big guys to get home. Just last night I fell asleep on the couch waiting for four kids to return home from a social event at Church. Because we live far out in the country, they don't get home until ten. Yep, I'd rather be snug as a bug in my bed, but I feel better waiting up in the living room (even if I'm dead asleep by then). I think they like knowing they'll find me there snoring.

And the day is done. I usually stumble back to sleep mumbling the Jesus Prayer ("Lord Jesus Christ, son of the living God, have mercy on me a sinner"), sometimes wondering if I use Jesus's name in prayer more as a sedative for myself than a true form of adoration.

The next day begins seven to eight hours later—at least for me. Ashley often has long nights, as mentioned.

This is how we do it. You will do it differently, I can almost guarantee. I'm convinced that there isn't a right or wrong way to perform specific activities on the operational level. It varies by situation. There is a lot of objective truth in life, but the perfect daily routine is not objective.

But there is an objective truth to an ordered family life.

You must be intentional about your routine if you want peace and unity within your family. You must build in time for winging it, but you cannot wing it every day.

"How do you manage fifteen children?" People ask me this all the time. Over the years, my answer has evolved. I have found the best and most accurate to be, "I don't. I manage systems and environments." And then this leads to a very interesting conversation.

Let me go ahead and make the obvious disclaimer: children are human beings, not widgets or units of production. Of course, I raise my children individually, as everyone must. Each and every one of them has different needs at different times. It is the job of my wife and I (and the older kids) to detect specific issues with specific kids and zoom in with love and affection—all other processes or systems be damned. Sometimes my world must stop and become nothing other than caring for a particular individual.

Good systems provide the freedom to zoom in like this with focus. In business, the purpose of good systems management (and the language that accompanies it) fosters even greater customized attention to each individual. Bad systems are stumbling blocks in business.

In family life, bad systems make it more difficult for Mom and Dad to pay close attention to particular kids (or each other) when the need arises.

SPAN OF CONTROL

We humans have a limited capacity to pay attention to items over a certain amount. When the items are people, they tend to blend into what we perceive as a group or crowd. We have trouble concentrating on items or managing people when presented with a long list. While the exact number may vary depending on the context and individual, it is commonly cited that the optimal span of control or attention for most people is around seven, plus or minus two. There's a reason why phone numbers are seven digits.

This principle is particularly important in life-threatening situations. Military squads, firefighting crews, police patrol units all pay close attention to the span of control of those in charge. Our minds begin to lose focus on units one through seven (for example) when unit eight is introduced. And as subsequent units are added, there is a precipitous drop in attention to the original seven. It's how we're wired.

When your kids are little, you exercise that span of control in a direct fashion. Your system is to keep your eyes fixed on them. Your system is to assign someone the direct task of babysitting when you have to leave. But the system is constant attention. Slowly, the attention level drops—or rather, expands to a larger perspective.

I had already studied this phenomenon when my eighth child was born, and I certainly enjoyed the jokes about forgetting the others existed! From a parenting standpoint, however, nature tends to take care of this issue.

By the time my eighth child was born, the older children no longer required the same level of attention a toddler does. You aren't overly concerned, for example, with your fourteen-year-old choking on a hotdog or running out into a busy street.

In business, you end up spreading your span of control over a larger number of people by mid-level management, delegation, and most importantly, systems.

SYSTEMS ALL THE WAY DOWN

In a well-ordered business, there are clearly documented systems for the areas of operation, such as manufacturing, recruiting and training, sales and marketing, warehousing and fulfillment, and accounting and finance. Moms and dads go out into the world every day and either manage these systems or operate within them. The average employee understands the importance of workflow, accountability, project management, and standard operating procedures whether they are an executive at Microsoft or a cook at McDonald's.

And yet, these same people return to their families and fail to bring their systems knowledge with them. Their families suffer from disorder and chaos. I think if moms and dads used their systems knowledge and experience in their families, home life would be easier and more rewarding. I can assure you that, as the father of fifteen, this has been my personal experience.

I started by asking myself, "Why am I so systems-oriented at work, but when I get home, I'm a sloppy, disheveled husband and father?" When I bring home my business competency to my family, my wife has a better partner, my kids enjoy a stronger father, and I feel more valuable because I have become more valuable.

So why don't we naturally do this?

A contrarian might respond, "Family isn't business. Spouses aren't colleagues. Children aren't employees." This is true. But it's also a lazy out. *Of course, families aren't businesses. This is simply an analogy.* But it's a powerful comparison.

Human beings live and thrive by metaphor. Conceptualization is largely a process of thinking via comparison and contrast. Every invention, every discovery, and every self-improvement has resulted from applying one set of knowledge, data, and experience to another pattern of facts. Without this ability, we would have never made it out of the cave—or never even survived in the cave for more than a generation. A useful comparison is not necessarily true in every detail. Instead, it is an analogy that works. And that is the value of applying business knowledge to family life. It works.

THE DEMING WAY

You might not know W. Edwards Deming, but you know his work. Have you ever said to your spouse, "Let's look into buying a Toyota because they last forever?" The reason Toyota has traditionally been a low-maintenance and long-lasting car is due to "The Deming Method." I'm convinced that the "Deming Method," Lean Management, Total Quality Management (TQM), and similar philosophies can dramatically increase the quality of your family life. Despite the increasing use of technology meant to simplify our lives, families have reached all-time levels of complexity; as businesses have grown in efficiency, families have grown in inefficiency. Family life appears to be suffering at the direct inverse of corporate America's streamlined corporate dynamism.

SYSTEMS THINKING

W. Edwards Deming (1900–1993) was an American statistician, engineer, and management consultant. Deming lectured in Japan in the 1950s on statistical quality control and management principles. His teachings and methods helped revolutionize Japanese manufacturing practices, contributing to their rise as a global economic powerhouse.[14]

Deming's principles, known as the "Deming Method,"[15] have had a profound impact on various industries worldwide, inspiring organizations to focus on quality, customer satisfaction, and long-term success. His work continues to be influential in the field of management and quality improvement.

Toyota adopted several of Deming's principles.

1. **Continuous Improvement:** Emphasizing the need for ongoing improvement in all areas of the organization.
2. **Statistical Process Control:** Using statistical techniques to monitor and control production processes.
3. **Employee Involvement:** Encouraging employees at all levels to contribute ideas and participate in problem-solving.
4. **Quality Management:** Prioritizing customer satisfaction and incorporating quality into all aspects of production.

Toyota implemented these principles into its production system and went on to become the first automobile manufacturer to produce more than ten million vehicles per year.[16] But what does this have to do with families?

---

14 Britannica, Editors of Encyclopaedia. "W. Edwards Deming." *Encyclopedia Britannica*, February 9, 2024. https://www.britannica.com/biography/W-Edwards-Deming.

15 "Dr. Deming's 14 Points for Management." The W. Edwards Deming Institute. https://deming.org /explore/fourteen-points/.

16 Takahashi, Yoshio. "Toyota Output Sets Industry Record," The Wall Street Journal, January 29, 2014. https://www.wsj.com/articles/SB10001424052702304428004579350030132963254.

PERFECTLY DESIGNED?

No system is perfectly designed, except from one standpoint: "Every system is perfectly designed to get the results it gets." This is one of Deming's most famous sayings. And I believe it applies particularly well to families.

As a consumer, you know a company's products are a direct reflection of its internal systems, processes, and organizational structure. If a company consistently achieves high levels of customer satisfaction and profitability, it is an indication that its systems and operations are effectively designed and operated. And the opposite is true, too. If a particular McDonald's routinely gets your order wrong, it's an indication of a poor system within the restaurant rather than just bad employees. The poor system leads to poor performance. Often good employees are as much the victims of a bad system as the customer.

Similarly, in other areas of life, such as personal development or health, the results we get are the outcomes of the systems or strategies we have in place. If you consistently practice healthy habits like exercise and balanced nutrition, you're more likely to achieve positive health outcomes. Conversely, if you don't have a well-designed system for time management and goal setting, you probably struggle to accomplish your objectives.

When you apply Deming's quote to family life, you see that the outcomes and dynamics we observe within our families are directly influenced by the systems we've established. If a family consistently enjoys open communication, strong relationships, and a harmonious environment, their systems for communication, conflict resolution, and quality time are effectively designed to foster those positive outcomes.

On the other hand, if a family experiences frequent conflicts or lack of connection, they need to evaluate and improve how they operate. Your frustrated family is very likely not a basket of bad apples! Instead, you are operating with a system perfectly designed to turn out loads of short-term fixes, scheduling bottlenecks, and general frustration instead of family harmony.

In essence, the Deming quote serves as a reminder that the results in any aspect of life, including family life, are not accidental but a reflection of the systems that are in place. It empowers us to take a closer look at our systems, make necessary adjustments, and intentionally design them to align with our desired outcomes and values.

YOU HAVE A SYSTEM FOR EVERYTHING

Everything in life is within a system whether you realize it or not.

I actually learned this underlying principle in a college classroom. The professor and class were talking about an artist who made national news for putting a crucifix in a jar of urine. This was supposed to be some form of high artistic expression. My classmates and I were appalled. I said, "This isn't even art!" And my professor wisely said, "No, Conor. It is art. It is just bad art." His answer has stayed with me.

So often we think we see the lack of something when we're actually seeing a bad version of that thing. When I began to study business systems, I heard so many people talking about the lack of systems. And I recollect that same notion I learned in the classroom: "No. There is a system. It's just a bad system."

This is the point I most want to get across. Whether you know it or not, you have a system for everything. You have a system for cooking and cleaning, for laundry, for budgeting and paying bills, for discipline. You have a digital media system. You have a conflict resolution system. And you have a prayer system.

You might say, "We have no budget! We just spend money blindly! So we don't have a budgeting system." Not so! Your system for budgets is to let nature take its course. That's your budgeting system!

If you don't regulate your teenager's smart phone, then your system is to entrust him with his phone and to trust the internet with your teenager. That's your system!

If you don't pray, then your prayer system is to simply trust your own best efforts in life and to believe that there is no need to build a personal relationship with God. That, my friends, is a system. It is a bad system. It is a dangerous system.

But don't be mistaken; it is a system.

BAD SYSTEM VS. GOOD PERSON

Deming also said, "A bad system will beat a good person every time." How true this is. I've seen many hardworking business owners crushed under the weight of their own poor systems. I've seen many hardworking parents crushed under the weight of their own poor family systems. Here's a good example, one you may be familiar with:

A young couple brings their two toddlers to church. They show up with a small arsenal of weapons in the diaper bag to fight off the temper tantrums: a bag of Cheerios, a toy car, a board book, sippy cups of juice. The parents' plan (or system) is to keep the kids completely occupied for the entire hour. And you know as well as I do that it rarely works.

The kids start to wiggle. Mom and Dad don't want to have a fight with the kids, so every few minutes they give them more and more room to move in the pew. Before long, one of the kids is running on the pew while the other kid has thrown Cheerios all over the place, dropped the sippy cup and let it roll under the pew in front, and torn a page from the hymnal.

So what does Dad do? He takes the kid running on the pew to the side aisle of the church so that the kid's feet are not making as much noise stomping about. It works for a moment because the kid has a slightly different environment. But within minutes, the kid is now running up and down the side aisle. The kid goes a little further each time. And then, as if out of the blue, the switch is flipped. Dad is done with the tomfoolery.

He chases down the kid who is almost to the altar. As Dad grabs an arm, the kid goes limp (as all kids do at that moment). Dad must scoop him up. The kid starts screaming and flailing about. Now Dad is really embarrassed and away they go to the narthex. Mom remains in the sanctuary and busily shovels Cheerios into the other kid's mouth. She eventually dishes out the toy car, which the kid pushes all across the pew while making engine noises, driving everyone around him crazy in the process.

And what do Mom and Dad say when they're socializing after church? "Well, my kids are just so strong-willed."

The above story might seem a little ridiculous. But I see some version of it most Sundays at church. And (while I'm not trying to brag), virtually every single Sunday, someone looks at us in marvel and says, "Your kids are so well-behaved!" We've even had a young mom (who really had no idea what she was doing or saying) comment about how lucky we were to have such naturally obedient children. Right. And fifteen times in a row.

Now that my mind has absorbed systems thinking, I look at the struggling couple with two little kids—two adults getting their butts kicked—and feel sorry for them. They are obviously loving and well-intentioned parents. They have their kids at church! That says something. But to my systems management mind, their poor systems are painfully obvious.

"A bad system will beat a good person every time." These parents' bad systems are crushing their good intentions and hard work.

While I'm not here to explain how to get kids to behave in a church pew, I do have a few points on the systems component. The parents' system was to give the kid room to move around. My system is to take as much room away as possible. *If you give a kid an inch, he will take a mile.* It is a bad system to let a kid move around too much in the pew. They need to sit and sit tight. I squish my toddler against the edge of the pew so they have very limited room. Why? Because if they move around on their fanny, they will get to their feet. If they get to their feet, they will walk on the pew. If they walk on the pew, they will run on the pew. Secondly, it is a poor system to bring food and drinks (admittedly, babies are different). You've just given the kid something to throw around, whether that's Cheerios or sippy cups. And it's a bad system to give your kids hymnals to play with. Eventually, they will rip the thin and fragile pages.

I could go on and on. But the point is simple: poor systems beat good parents every time.

I could have just as easily given the not-so-harmless story of good parents inadvertently allowing their teenagers to watch pornography on their phones in their room alone simply because of poor digital systems in the house. We will return to this issue shortly.

SYSTEMS CREATE FREEDOM

The result of a good system is not only a good product or service but freedom itself. I've experienced this both at work and in the family. A good system creates many types of freedom, including freedom of time, freedom of organization, and freedom of the mind.

    1. Freedom of Time: Efficient systems help parents save time by streamlining routines and processes. This allows them to have more time for themselves, their children, and activities they enjoy. It is inefficient systems that cause conflict and confusion, ultimately resulting in cluttered activity. That is, unless failure and disorganized commotion are what you are seeking. In that case, those systems are perfectly efficient for churning out dysfunction!

2. **Freedom of Organization:** Systems enable parents to stay organized and reduce chaos. By establishing systems for managing schedules, household tasks, and paperwork, parents can experience a sense of freedom in maneuvering through their daily tasks. This may seem counterintuitive at first glance, but it's true! Spontaneity and freedom of action increase exponentially when your life is properly organized.

3. **Freedom of the Mind:** Well-designed systems alleviate mental burdens and help parents feel more at ease. When parents don't have to constantly worry about managing every aspect of family life, they invariably experience a greater sense of peace and mental well-being.

One definition of stress is simply this: stress is thinking about something when you don't want to. Without efficient systems, your own thoughts and emotions never get a chance to settle. They swim around with every tide pushing and pulling them. But when you live by systems, you have a sense of peace knowing that things will be thought about, discussed, and handled at the right time, in the right place, with the right people.

SYSTEM BREAKDOWN

A system refers to the framework of interconnected components working toward a common goal. In the following chapters, I break down systems for your family into two categories: environments and processes.

Environments are macrosystems, the larger communities your family participates in—school, sports, social groups, church life, and so on. As a parent, you're outsourcing much of your child's spiritual, emotional, physical, and mental development to these environments—not unlike a business that outsources certain product development to specialists outside of the company. You should look upon these environments as outsourced suppliers, vendors, and consultants. If you don't trust them, change them. But I want to help you see the interconnectedness of your child's different environments forming a unique ecosystem in which your child thrives or declines. Your child truly does live in a vast garden—curated and tended by you. In my opinion, this is the single greatest failure of modern parenting—namely, not appreciating and/or managing the interconnected environments that shape the characters of children.

Processes are the second, smaller variety of system. These microsystems are more localized, more detailed, and operate within a shorter time frame. Some would say numerous processes make up a system. It's more accurate to see them as systems within systems, like the gears in a transmission. In family life, I am using the term *process* for those smaller controls that help your day-to-day life, such as chore charts, morning and evening routines, prayer routines, and so on.

In the end, the following chapters are meant to bring into focus the macrosystems (environments) and microsystems (processes) that are currently having massive impacts on your family life, whether you realize it or not. I'm here to tell you that improving these systems is largely within your control.

But first, let's take a moment to consider *where* all these systematic processes occur. An ocean wave cannot exist without the sea through which it moves, the winds that shape it, and the tidal fluxes induced by the Moon.

And a family system can only exist within a family's environments.

"Fish don't know they're in water."

—ANONYMOUS

CHAPTER

7

ENVIRONMENTS

MOMMA BEARS AND ASSEMBLY LINES

Women, by nature, have an intuition that men can only dream of. Men usually need data to solve a problem. Women just need exposure to the situation. (Of course, I am speaking in generalities and from my own perception. Obviously, this doesn't apply to everyone.)

There is an important point here for parents. Men, by nature, are more inclined toward systems. They build great assembly lines. They form and function well within a militaristic structure. If both Mom and Dad learn to see the family as operating within larger systems, I believe the woman's natural instincts of intuition and protection and the man's natural abilities

to form and function within an overarching system will not only coexist but flourish.

As your children leave the nest, you are not sending them out into a void. Rather, you are sending them out into predefined environments with clear attributes and levels of influence on particularly young and impressionable souls. You are, in effect, outsourcing portions of your child's development to these external environments. And there is no way around this.

When you think of it this way, you might start asking yourself a different set of questions. *Would I outsource my child's social development to social media outlets? Would I trust my son's travel soccer team to teach him about sexual morality? Would I trust the public schools to teach my daughter about gender identity? Would I trust the entertainment industry to teach my son about God and politics?*

I'm not suggesting we can or should escape all aspects of the world around us. We all know the overly protective parent who micro-manages every aspect of his or her child's life. In my experience, this is usually the result of an overbearing mother and a weak-willed or absent father. No offense to moms! It is, in fact, in your nature to protect your young from the dangerous environment more than it is instinctive within dads. There's a reason we say "momma bear" when someone messes with a mother's child. I've never heard a reference to "daddy bear." The same holds true with birds in a nest, or puppies in a litter, or chimps in a troop.

Not only do moms have a defensive instinct, but moms are naturally conditioned (thank you, God) with an enhanced awareness of approaching danger. I would trust Mom's assessment of a stranger long before I would trust Dad's.

It happens practically every day. By now, I'm used to it. Ashley's intuition is so strong that I barely notice it. She will make a pronouncement from out of the blue like, "Did you notice something is wrong with [insert child's name]?"

And I will answer along the lines of, "Is he even home? I haven't seen him."

"We just had dinner with him, Conor!"

"Oh, um. Well. Is he sick or something?"

And then she will explain that he's acting distant or lethargic or in some other uncharacteristic manner. "You need to go talk to him."

And when I do so I learn that, yep, something was definitely wrong.

How did Ashley notice? I have no idea. Her intuition helps me be a better father.

Or, I'll say, "Let's watch that movie. I loved this one when I was a kid!" All I have is good memories of the film.

And then Ashley will point out that I probably saw it when I was a teenager and more mature than my proposed audience. There are quasi-raunchy scenes in it along with foul language and foul humor. Am I really so sure this is the movie for us to watch?

Before, I had zero memory of this in my nostalgic recollection of the film, but when I think about it a moment, I recall everything about this so-called harmless movie that I would *never* want my seven-year-old to see. Nope. No way!

I am always surprised when this sort of thing pops up. Would I have sat there and watched the film with them, then kicked myself afterward? Probably. But luckily, I have a woman's intuition on the prowl only a couple of feet away from me.

Ashley can hear a cry and know whether the kid bumped his head or scratched his knee. I don't even hear the noise. The first sound I hear is Ashley's voice, "Conor! Engage!"

And then I pull myself to at least a motley sort of attention and recollect what's going on that I have not registered.

Another example. We have a sick kid. We pick up a prescription from Walgreens. I get home and start to give the meds to the kid, following the instructions. Ashley stops me and says, "Let's check the dosage." She double checks and discovers that the bottle is labeled as requiring the medicine be dispensed in *tablespoons* when she knows the dosage is supposed to be in *teaspoons*.

The pharmacist put it in wrong. I would have overdosed my kid!

How could anybody have known that?

Yet Ashley does.

I would have just followed the instructions on the bottle. But for Momma Bear, arbitrary directions are not good enough. She lives in a state of constant awareness and protective alertness when it comes to her baby cubs. As for me, I often sit on the sidelines like a baboon scratching my head.

I don't think I am alone in this. I believe most dads might identify with this dynamic. Mom has a sixth sense. I'm lucky to have five senses active at once. She has an ability to detect a threat and to focus on that threat no matter what is going on. I'm supremely grateful for this ability. Of course, it isn't just an instinct. Her innate faculty is perfected by constant effort and selfless love—as well as by years of experience.

The bottom line is that there may be more environments at work on your family than you realize, some you may not even be directly aware of with your limited perspective. Yet it is important to identify these and contemplate the impact they have on your family.

The Family STRREP Test™ can help.

THE FAMILY STRREP TEST™

In the business world, the PESTLE analysis is a popular strategic tool used to assess external factors that can influence an organization's performance. It examines six key categories: Political, Economic, Social, Technological, Legal, and Environmental. By analyzing these factors, businesses can understand potential risks and opportunities in the market and make informed decisions to adapt their strategies accordingly.

As I learned to use this tool in my corporate life, it became obvious that many of the same external factors related to my family life. As I focused on those external environments that most affect family life, I repeatedly observed the influences that most families confront with little kids. These influences presented themselves in similar form over and over again. They were so regular that you might even create a short mnemonic for them. So I did. And thus, The Family STRREP Test™ diagnosis tool was born.

Just as strep throat is a bacterial infection, the environments that attack your family can be bacterial infections for the soul. On the other hand, there is nothing more valuable than wholesome external environments.

STRREP is an acronym for the external factors that influence your family.

- **S**ocial
- **T**echnological
- **R**ecreational
- **R**eligious
- **E**ducational
- **P**rofessional

Social[17]

> "Man, when perfected, is the best of animals,
> but when separated from law and justice,
> he is the worst of all."
>
> *—Aristotle*

The first letter in STRREP gets at the very essence of human nature. Each member of your family is a "social animal." How do all those external environments positively or negatively impact your family? Are there friendships that are negatively impacting your teenager? Are there neighbors that are a bad influence on your elementary school kid? Is there extended family that is creating stress in your marriage?

Imagine an average German boy in the 1930s raised in a solidly religious family with an excellent education and wholesome friendships. In a few short years after his innocent boyhood and experience of a loving family, he becomes a Nazi soldier. He may even have become one of the guards who led countless human beings, stripped of clothes and dignity, into a gas chamber. What happened to this innocent young boy? Or are we to believe that hundreds of thousands of young men and women of the Nazi party were raised around dinner tables of wrath and received their First Communions in sanctuaries of sadism?

A famous experiment illustrates just how susceptible humans are to social factors.

The Milgram Experiment

Yale psychologist Dr. Stanly Milgram proved that within minutes, the average person would succumb to social pressures and perceived authority figures and be willing to do the unimaginable.

---

17 For an in-depth analysis of your child's God-given social nature, the three types of friendships, and how to raise your child in a social media world, see part 2 of my book, *If Aristotle's Kid Had an iPod: Ancient Wisdom for Modern Parents* (Saint Benedict Press, 2012).

The experiments were initiated in July 1961, a year following the trial of Adolf Eichmann, the notorious Nazi soldier responsible for countless deaths. During his trial in Jerusalem, Eichmann, like other Nuremberg Trial defendants, claimed he was merely following orders from his superiors, including Hitler.[18]

Just months after receiving his PhD from Harvard, Milgram assumed a professorship at Yale and began conducting experiments to investigate whether ordinary individuals would be willing to administer lethal electric shocks to innocent strangers. Participants, who were recruited through newspaper ads for a study on learning, were paid $4.50 per hour.

The participants were instructed to ask questions to test subjects seated behind a wall and connected to electrical wires. Incorrect answers prompted the questioners to administer electrical zaps, with the voltage increasing for each wrong response. The results were shocking, to say the least.

Hearing the subjects scream in pain, many questioners pleaded to end the experiment, protested its fairness, and showed signs of remorse. Nevertheless, a single man, an "authority figure" dressed in a white coat, would calmly instruct, "Please sit down and read the next question. The test must go on." The questioners would repeatedly violate their conscience and continue shocking the man (even though the victim was an actor and received no actual shocks). This demonstrated how ordinary people, influenced by authority figures, could go against their conscience, akin to what Nazi soldiers did during their atrocities.

Parents, I implore you to internalize this as a warning. Our children are not morally bulletproof. Be fully aware that your child and your family are susceptible to external factors. We can never let down our guard. Remember, "A bad system will beat a good person every time." A bad social system will beat a good child, a good woman, or a good man every time. Be vigilant and build your family systems around a morally sound social life.

And modern social life includes plenty of technological factors as well.

---

18 Abbott, Alison. "Modern Milgram Experiment Sheds Light on Power of Authority." Nature News, February 18, 2016. https://www.nature.com/articles/nature.2016.19408.

Technological

Nearly five billion people use social media for an average of more than two and a half hours a day.[19] What is the technological environment in which your family lives? Think about the impact of the digital world on your family: smartphones, internet, social media, video streaming services, and so on. It is vitally important to assess how these factors are affecting your family, particularly your children—and *especially* your teenagers.

The average teenager spends more than seven hours *per day* on a screen.[20]

If asked, can you say exactly what your digital policy is for your kids? If you're like most, the answer is most definitely no.

For now, ask yourself: What is your family screentime? How many hours a day is your teenager on her smartphone? How many texts? How many Instagram reels? How many TikTok videos? How many . . . how many . . . how many? All these technologies form your child's environment.

Is the smartphone interfering with conversations? What's your kid being exposed to and for how many hours a day? In the next chapter, I will help you in crafting and implementing a Family Digital Policy. For now, just consider the first concerns that come to mind. There are positive aspects to consider too. Does texting enable you to stay in communication with your college student? Has technology made it easier to homeschool? Can your family stream wholesome programs rather than channel surf through the muck of cable TV?

Recreational

Recreational environments include those focused on physical activities, such as sports, outdoor activities, music and the arts, and other hobbies. These "leisure" activities often become anything but that.

Have sports overtaken your family life? Are you too busy driving to baseball and soccer fields to have family dinner? Are you missing church to travel with the softball team? Are your kids being negatively influenced, season after

---

19 "50+ of the most important social media marketing statistics for 2023," Sprout Social, March 23, 2023, https://sproutsocial.com/insights/social-media-statistics/.

20 Fabio Duarte, "Average Screen Time for Teens (2023)," Exploding Topics, April 9, 2023, https://exploding topics.com/blog/screen-time-for-teens.

season, by the kids on their teams? Have music lessons become drudgery? Or do you find sports, music, and outdoor activities beneficial to your family life? Do you notice that playing sports helps your child become disciplined and the environment is truly uplifting?

The main question you must ask yourself is this: Are recreational activities actually benefitting the soul of your child and the spirit of your family? If the answer is no, then you must develop a plan to alter your recreational system to better support your vision for your family.

Religious

The religious environment outside the family is the most important factor affecting your family's spiritual life. If you have a vibrant church community, you are more likely to pray as a family in the home, Mom and Dad are more likely to have uplifting friendships, and the kids are more likely to develop friendships that provide an escape from modern secularism.

A 2018 Harvard study on children found that regular churchgoers reported higher happiness levels, joined in more community causes, and stayed away from more illicit drugs than their non-religious peers.[21] A 1994 Swiss study showed the biggest impact on a child's future church attendance was the father's church attendance.[22]

How is your religious life affecting your family? Is there any part of it that you want to bolster? Might you need to change churches to experience a greater benefit for your entire family? Are there practical ways you can get more involved at church?

As Catholics, my family tries to live out the liturgical calendar by incorporating various seasons and feasts of the Church into our daily lives. The liturgical calendar is, among other things, a system provided by the Church to bring order and clarity into our lives and day-to-day activities.

---

21 Chris Sweeney, "Religious upbringing linked to better health and well-being during early adulthood," Harvard T. H. Chan School of Public Health, September 13, 2018, https://www.hsph.harvard.edu/news/press-releases/religious-upbringing-adult-health/.

22 Dean Smith, "Swiss study shows fathers are important to a child's church attendance," OpentheWord, June 16, 2014, https://openheword.org/2014/06/16/swiss-study-shows-fathers-are-important-to-a-childs-church-attendance/.

- **Advent:** During Advent, the family lights the Advent wreath candles each week. A family can read daily Advent reflections or Scriptures together and participate in special prayers or activities to prepare for the celebration of Christmas. Traditionally, Advent is a penitential season. Just as you might "give up" something in Lent, you should consider doing the same in Advent.[23]
- **Christmas:** On Christmas Day, the family attends Mass together to celebrate the birth of Jesus. Families should also exchange gifts, have a special Christmas dinner, and focus on the true meaning of Christmas as the birth of Christ.
- **Lent:** During Lent, the family might participate in the Stations of the Cross, practice fasting or abstinence on Fridays, and engage in acts of charity or service to others.
- **Easter:** On Easter Sunday, the family can attend a joyful Easter Mass, have an Easter egg hunt, and gather for a festive meal to celebrate the resurrection of Jesus.
- **Feast Days:** Families can mark the feast days of various saints throughout the liturgical year by attending Mass on those days, learning about the lives of the saints, and incorporating special prayers or traditions related to each saint. In the Gallagher house, we often use these feast days as a little excuse to enjoy some special treats. Even during Advent and Lent, we soften up the sacrifices on the feast days of our kids' saints.

These are just a few examples of how a family can live out the liturgical calendar, integrating faith and worship into their daily lives to build a strong foundation for spiritual growth and understanding within the family unit. My family does plenty of this, but there is more we could do.

The point is to form your own cohesive religious environment where your family lives and operates. If religion is a mere task to be performed, it will never take root.

---

23 In the past, Advent was a solemn and penitential season, emphasizing the preparation for the celebration of Christ's birth. It focused on reflection, fasting, and spiritual readiness. However, in modern times, the true meaning of Advent has been overshadowed by the commercialization of Christmas, transforming it into a pre-Christmas period. With the increasing emphasis on gift-giving, decorations, and festivities, the original penitential nature of Advent has been diluted. Traditionally, the twelve days of Christmas would begin on Christmas Day, with celebrations extending beyond December 25. Saying Merry Christmas before the actual day was uncommon, reflecting a reverence for the sacred event. The old way was better . . . if you ask me.

And do you see church as a duty or a privilege? Have you told your children that many people around the world don't have religious liberty? You don't have to attend church underground. You don't have to hide your Bible. How can you capitalize on these liberties to build a beautiful environment where your family's spiritual life can thrive?

Educational

The educational environments are particularly impactful on your family because they become an epicenter for the other factors. The school system in which your family operates often drives the social, technological, and recreational environments. This can be great if the educational system is strong and wholesome. This can be tragic if it's a product of modern secularism.

Consider everything about the educational environment in which your family operates, including the teachers, the students, the curricula, and the positive or negative influences of the administration.

If you homeschool as we do, consider whether you have the proper number of co-ops or other networks for classes. At times, we've lacked sufficient class options for our kids. At other times, we've been overly busy with too many classes for our kids in different locations. It's a hard balance to strike. And it's a system that must be reviewed each year.

No matter your schooling status, consider the pros and cons of your current situation and brainstorm on how this can be improved. Much more is in your control than you might think.

Professional

The professional work environments include both the work environment of the parents and of the working teenagers. Both external factors heavily influence the family. Does Mom or Dad have a job that really brings them down? Is the stress of Dad's job negatively affecting Mom's mood with the kids? Is Mom juggling too many balls trying to work part-time while raising the kids—but the money is really needed?

Mom and Dad most likely discuss the pros and cons of their own employment regularly. But if you have teenagers, are they working in proper environments? Are they developing life-skills and learning to experience the "real world" in a positive way? Or are their coworkers unnecessarily exposing them to the nasty side of the world? Perhaps the exposure is too much and too soon. We've experienced both positive and negative work environments for our teenagers. It's stressful as a parent to help your teenagers maneuver through the world without jeopardizing their own well-being. Ashley and I talk about this all the time. These questions must be asked by Mom and Dad as they allow the teenager to test the waters of the professional world.

Now that we've looked at each individual category, it's time to take a close look at The Family STRREP Test™. On the follwing page, you will see a sample test.

In this example, five of the six categories fall into the 8–11 range. For those five categories, the family should consider how to optimize those environments and monitor them closely for either positive or negative changes. Immediate action is likely unnecessary.

But the score of 7 in the Social category warrants special attention. The family should make a plan and take action soon to avoid or minimize any negative impact of neighbors moving away and the influence of untrustworthy older cousins.

Now it's time for you to take your own Family STRREP Test™. Remember to prayerfully consider these external environments and how they impact your family life and the individual lives of family members.

Total up your scores in each category. Make a plan for change where necessary. Brainstorm about ways to optimize an environment even if it might not be a category that merits immediate action. If your scores are high, clarify exactly the reasons why, look for anything you might be missing, and continue to strive to foster improved environments.

Before celebrating your achievements or lamenting your shortcomings, stand back from your immediate viewpoint and consider how you would advise *another* family with similar results, issues, or challenges as yours. Most of all, be honest with your assessment and move forward with a resolve and conviction about doing what is best for your family.

THE FAMILY STRREP TEST™

Instructions: For each category, write down the three most impactful factors for your family.
Rank each 1-5: 1-Major Threat, 2-Moderate Threat, 3-Neutral, 4-Moderate Plus, 5-Major Plus
Add the three scores from each category for total category score.

Category	Three Most Impactful Factors	Rank 1-5	Total
SOCIAL	New friends for middle schoolers.	3	7
	Untrustworthy older cousins.	2	
	Neighbor friends moved away.	2	
TECHNOLOGICAL	Time on phone for parents after kids are in bed.	2	9
	New wholesome streaming option.	5	
	Screen time for kids.	2	
RECREATIONAL	Practice time interfering with schoolwork.	1	9
	Music lessons.	5	
	Watching football games on TV.	3	
RELIGIOUS	New pastor at church.	3	10
	Current church vs. possible new one.	3	
	Youth group activities.	4	
EDUCATIONAL	Long commutes to school interfering with family time.	2	8
	Lack of parental involvement in high school.	3	
	Frustrating teachers.	3	
PROFESSIONAL	Dad's work schedule is relatively flexible.	5	9
	Mom stressed about online business.	1	
	Long-term career plans not obvious.	3	

GRADING SCALE: The categories with the lowest scores deserve the most attention.

Guidelines for category total scores within these ranges:

3-7: Make a plan for environmental changes. Take action immediately or in the near future.

8-11: Consider how to optimize environments. Continue to monitor closely.

12-15: Continue to foster environments. Consult others for anything you might be missing.

THE FAMILY STRREP TEST™

Instructions: For each category, write down the three most impactful factors for your family.
Rank each 1-5: 1-Major Threat, 2-Moderate Threat, 3-Neutral, 4-Moderate Plus, 5-Major Plus
Add the three scores from each category for total category score.

Category	Three Most Impactful Factors	Rank 1-5	Total
SOCIAL			
TECHNOLOGICAL			
RECREATIONAL			
RELIGIOUS			
EDUCATIONAL			
PROFESSIONAL			

GRADING SCALE: The categories with the lowest scores deserve the most attention.

Guidelines for category total scores within these ranges:

3-7: Make a plan for environmental changes. Take action immediately or in the near future.

8-11: Consider how to optimize environments. Continue to monitor closely.

12-15: Continue to foster environments. Consult others for anything you might be missing.

FAMILY ECOSYSTEMS

The STRREP external factors are interrelated. They form an interconnected ecosystem influencing a family, especially the children's development. It's crucial for parents to recognize how each environment impacts *other* aspects of the family's life and to manage that group of factors holistically. As we review each individual environment, think about them as a system of gears interconnected as one ecosystem creating the momentum for your family's path in life.

- **Social Environment:** Relationships with extended family, friends, and the community at large directly influence a child's expectations of the other external factors. More areas of your child's life will be impacted by his social circles than perhaps any other.
- **Technological Environment:** Digital influence affects communication, education, and recreation, requiring responsible digital behavior for balanced family interactions.
- **Recreational Environment:** Shared leisure activities strengthen family relationships, creating emotional support within the family. But obsessive focus on sports or negative influences on the field or in the locker rooms can have monumental impacts on the other areas of your child's life.
- **Religious Environment:** Perhaps more than any other, religious environments form a child's moral foundation. Parents should work extremely hard to allow social, recreational, and even educational benefits to spill out of the religious environments into the other environments.
- **Educational Environment:** The educational system is the main factor that produces the social and technological environments in which your kid operates. Parents can't deprogram kids in a few hours a day after they have been programmed for eight to ten hours a day in school. Make sure the "programming" is what you want.
- **Professional/Work Environment:** A parent's job affects both parents' stress level, work-life balance, and availability for family, influencing overall family well-being. Likewise, the teenager's work environment will often produce friendships the parent is not even aware of. Know that it isn't just a paycheck the teenager is picking up from work.

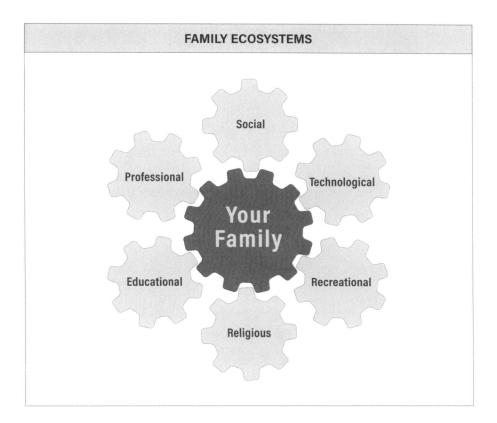

FAMILY ECOSYSTEMS

As the world becomes more and more perverse and disordered, some families have gone to great lengths to create customized family ecosystems that protect their family members (not just the kids).

One interesting and well-known concept related to this is "The Benedict Option" as proposed by Rod Dreher in his book of the same name.[24] It suggests that Christians, feeling marginalized in a secularizing society, should respond by withdrawing to intentional, close-knit communities centered around shared religious beliefs and practices. Modeled after the monastic lifestyle of St. Benedict, this approach seeks to preserve and strengthen traditional Christian values, culture, and faith in a challenging and rapidly changing world.

---

24 Dreher, Rod. *The Benedict Option: A Strategy for Christians in a Post-Christian Nation*. New York, NY: Sentinel, 2018.

The idea is to create a countercultural, self-sustaining community that fosters spiritual growth, moral living, and resilience in the face of secular influences.

In other words, to withdraw from damaging ecosystems and build new ones. Such a radical approach might have seemed quirky or even benighted a couple of decades ago. These days it merits serious consideration.

CONCLUSION

To recap, recognizing the interconnectedness of external environments enables parents to nurture a positive ecosystem—the macrosystem in which your family operates. Learn to see the macrosystem of your family life. These are like gears, all interconnected, turning round and round, producing the family that you are.

Going forward, keep in mind W. Edward Deming's two most famous quotes.

1. "Every system is perfectly designed to get the results that it gets."
2. "A bad system will beat a good person every time."

It may sound overly judgmental, but I would say that parents spend too much time focused on the individual and not enough time on the environment of the individual and the ecosystem of the family. I've seen the same in business.

I've observed the company that has a terrible culture with the leader focusing energy and effort on a few individual all-star salespeople. The hubris in such corporate leaders is the same hubris in parents; namely, they think their own leadership or relationship with the individual can "beat" the environment. In the short run, maybe it can. In the long run, it can't.

"A bad system will beat a good person every time." As true today as when Deming's methods were applied to the Toyota manufacturing process. And the rest is history.

After having worked through this chapter, you are more equipped to answer for yourself a question very few ask themselves: *What is the system my family has designed for itself on the macrolevel?*

And once you see the big picture, you start making simple, practical changes that make day-to-day life a little easier.

This is where everything gets better—systematically.

8

PROCESSES

It was only after I studied the art and science of systems that I began to see the microsystems, or processes, in every single aspect of life. They are so essential that if we paid attention to them during normal activity, we would not be able to move seamlessly from one action to another. If you think about the process of taking a breath every time you breathe, you're likely to pass out from lack of oxygen. Or hyperventilate.

We previously spoke of macrosystems, or environments, those larger structures and communities in which your family operates. Here, we will focus on those smaller systems that we call processes.

Let's define our terms. A process is a series of actions, steps, or operations that are undertaken to achieve a specific outcome or goal. It involves the systematic and organized execution of tasks in a prescribed sequence or order. The purpose of a process is to streamline and optimize the execution of tasks, ensuring efficiency, effectiveness, and consistency in achieving the proper objectives.

YOUR FAMILY PROCESSES

Think about all the processes in which you have worked, that you have studied, or have experienced. The first step to implementing improved processes in your family life is to appreciate how processes have determined success, failure, or frustration in so many other areas of your life.

Now turn to your family. Let's start with a simple list. Let me help you with that. See how many well-defined, carefully structured processes are involved in just making breakfast for the kiddos in the morning.

- **Morning routine:** alarm clock sounds, make the coffee, brush your teeth.
- **Getting kids ready for school:** wake the kids, get them dressed, feed them breakfast, pack their lunch, get in the car.
- **Breakfast:** keep the cereal in the pantry, keep milk in the fridge, keep the bowls in the cabinet, keep the spoons in the drawer.
- **Driving to the grocery store:** grab the car keys from the key hook next to the garage, unlock the car, buckle your seat belt, use turn signals, follow speed limits, stop at red lights, go at green lights.
- **Buying milk:** grab a cart sitting for you at the entrance, walk to the dairy section, go to the milk section within the diary section, choose the self-checkout, type your PIN, take your receipt.

Each time you pour milk into a bowl of cereal, it's the result of hundreds or even thousands of beautifully managed processes. Just ask a dairy farmer about his processes. They are meticulous. Ask the wheat farmer who helped make the cereal. His processes are staggering in complexity. Ask the grocery store manager about the processes he must oversee every day to stock the shelves. Think about the processes keeping the roads safe so you can drive to the grocery store. And lastly, think about the processes you have in your own home so that you can effectively pour milk into a bowl once you bring that cereal home! As simple as it sounds, making a bowl of cereal is the outcome of a system. Your kitchen is organized in a particular way for a particular reason.

Why don't you keep your cereal bowls in the refrigerator with the milk? Because your process says they go in the cupboard. Why don't you just pour out all the cereal into the silverware drawer? Because your system says to use a bowl.

Every aspect of our lives is covered by process. Look around. See it. Love it. And the better you get at seeing it, the better you will be at intentionally building new and better processes to help your family thrive.

Below is a list of processes that you likely use in your life. Some of these you intentionally manage, others simply happen according to some sort of plan, if not yours. Check all that apply.

- ☐ **Morning Routine:** Getting up, brushing teeth, showering, and getting ready for the day
- ☐ **Commuting:** Traveling to work or school using various transportation methods
- ☐ **Work/School Routine:** Engaging in daily tasks, meetings, classes, and assignments
- ☐ **Meal Preparation:** Planning, shopping, cooking, and eating meals
- ☐ **Financial Management:** Budgeting, paying bills, and managing expenses
- ☐ **Social Interactions:** Communicating with family, friends, and colleagues
- ☐ **Time Management:** Organizing and prioritizing daily activities and tasks
- ☐ **Exercise and Fitness:** Engaging in physical activities or going to the gym
- ☐ **Sleep Routine:** Preparing for sleep and maintaining a regular sleep schedule
- ☐ **Household Chores:** Cleaning, laundry, and maintaining the living space
- ☐ **Health Maintenance:** Going for regular check-ups, doctor visits, and taking medications
- ☐ **Decision Making:** Making choices and problem-solving in daily life
- ☐ **Technology Usage:** Interacting with computers, smartphones, and other devices
- ☐ **Shopping:** Buying groceries, clothes, and other necessities
- ☐ **Personal Development:** Pursuing hobbies, learning new skills, and self-improvement
- ☐ **Social Media:** Engaging with online platforms for entertainment and information
- ☐ **Personal Relationships:** Nurturing and maintaining connections with family and friends
- ☐ **Goal Setting:** Setting short-term and long-term objectives for personal growth

All of these are processes. In other words, these activities don't occur randomly. For example, you may not have an exact bedtime, but you probably go to bed every night within a ninety-minute window. You might not feel that you have a meal prep process, but more than likely there are a handful of meals and take-out restaurants you rely on, and I'll wager your pantry is filled with 80 percent of the same contents on any given day. We all have our "go-tos," our "usuals." These are the result of processes.

In the space below, list areas of your life where you have operated within a predefined system. Describe what was good, helpful, or positive about this system. What made it a good system that enabled success?

KFPs

Now that we have considered the general processes in which you live, let's focus on the most important processes in your family life. We will call these KFPs for Key Family Processes.

This is *it*. This is the Big Kahuna of Process I have to lay on you.

The Key Family Process — the KFP — is at the heart of every family system. KFPs are the bones in the skeleton, the notes in the symphony.

This is where your journey starts. So let's get down to business. Family business.

Well-run businesses are wise to have a master list of their most essential processes, their "core processes," or key processes. This may consist of a dozen processes that drive the most critical parts of the business. In my business, this includes lead generation, email marketing, social media marketing, digital ads, customer journey, editorial and production, inventory analysis and procurement, fulfillment, customer service, and payables and receivables. Each of these processes needs a distinct name and a defined process. A defined process should be nothing more than a list of bulleted steps (we will discuss below how detailed this should be).

So many businesses take this for granted. The general feeling, particularly in a legacy business, is "We know our most important processes like the back of our hands!" And when you ask them to name them, you sit back and listen to a convoluted mishmash of how their business sort of operates. In fact, start-ups often have a humility (sometimes rooted in fear of failure)

Example

PROCESS	POSITIVE ATTRIBUTES
P90x3 Workout Routine	- Provided calendar of workouts - Following video helps me stay on pace
Automatic drafts	- Eliminates steps of writing checks - Easier to budget and track expenses - Easier to automate paying off debt
Curriculum for kids	- Keeps them moving at a good pace - Reduces preparation time for teachers
Project software	- Keeps assigned parties and dates in front of the team - Cuts down on conflict over details - Reduces rework and waiting time

PROCESS	POSITIVE ATTRIBUTES

that warmly welcomes the need to document their core processes. The same goes for families: the older, more experienced families are often resistant to an exercise like this, while a younger family is still excited and desires to shape the best possible future.

In the business world, the acronyms KPIs (Key Performance Indicators) and KRAs (Key Result Areas) are well-known.[25] These acronyms make communication easy. Think about making KFPs part of your family lexicon. You can easily say, "Things seem really chaotic right now. Let's look at our KFPs to see if anything is out of whack." Or, you might say, "We need to add a smartphone docking process to our KFPs." It's a lot easier to use the acronym than saying Key Family Process every time.

KFP, KFP, KFP . . .

What are your KFPs? I recommend three to five. If you have more than five, you might be going beyond the "key" processes. While a business might have twelve or more, a family isn't a business (this is an analogy!) and needs greater simplicity.

Some examples of KFPs (and their purposes) could include:

- **Morning routines:** wake up times, coffee and breakfast, getting the day going
- **Evening routines:** bath times for little ones, prayers, getting ready for bed
- **Family Prayer:** when and how your family comes together in prayer
- **Chores:** who does what chores on each day of the week
- **Schoolwork:** consistent times and places set for doing homework every day
- **Household finances:** planning a family budget, sticking to it, and reviewing it
- **Smartphone policy:** creating guidelines, setting schedules, and safety measures

---

25 To avoid confusion, KRAs and KPIs are not synonymous with core processes, nor are they synonymous with each other. Key Result Areas are those areas within an organization that are critical to achieving strategic goals. Key Performance Indicators are metrics used to evaluate an activity to further strategic goals. For example, a KRA might be "Boost Brand Awareness." The KPIs for this might be the metrics of (1) website traffic, (2) social media engagement, and (3) number of leads generated.

- **Meal planning:** planning ahead meals, shopping lists, snacking prohibitions
- **Family Meeting Cadence:** establishing the rhythm and content of your family meetings

The KFP Finalizer™ is a tool to help you brainstorm concerning the many processes that your family currently follows, even if imperfectly. This tool will help you to sort through your list and select your KFPs.

This is where your family life begins to change for the better. Sharpen a pencil. Put on your thinking cap. Use the worksheet if that seems helpful. Do whatever it takes. Make the list. Edit. Combine. Revise. Define your KFPs.

More progress! You now have Key Family Processes clearly articulated and mapped out. Keep in mind that none of this is set in stone. Your KFPs will change over time. Children age. Life circumstances go through cycles. Some days it rains, some days the wind blows. As your family goes through stages of growth, the processes to focus on should also change. Don't hesitate to call an audible and turn your family's focus to a different process.

One thing to remember: make sure to avoid having a huge list of processes. No family member wants to feel like they live on an assembly line. The family is not a business. It just behaves like one most of the time!

A NOTE ON UNIQUENESS

My friend works in the private school system for elementary grades. He tells a funny story. Each school year, the moms, one by one, pull the teacher to the side and say, "I just thought I should explain to you that my little Sally is special. She is *particularly* gifted. She was reading when she was three years old. I just want her to get the attention she deserves." The joke is that the teacher then looks at the mom and says, "That's great! She will fit right into this class because apparently *all* of them are special and gifted." Sometimes the moms laugh. Sometimes they don't find this revelation very amusing at all.

THE KFP FINALIZER™

STEP ONE: List those areas of life that are both (a) recurring and (b) benefit from guidelines, rules, or routines.

- Morning routines	- Evening routines	- Taking care of grandma
- Inside chores	- Prayers	- Weekend excursions
- Outside chores	- To and from sports	- Gardening
- Getting schoolwork done	- Cell phone control	- Cleaning out the cars
- Paying the bills	– Meal prep	- Taking care of animals

STEP TWO: Pick the three to five areas of life above that make the biggest impact on your long-term family goals. Write down what makes these areas so important.

Area of Life	Why this area has significant impact on your long-term family goals
Inside chores	- A messy house brings stress to Mom and Dad. - Kids need to appreciate their belongings and clean up after themselves. - Assigned tasks will cut down on fighting over who does what.
Cell phone control	- It is vital to keep kids away from inappropriate images and videos. -Too much screen time causes anxiety and division in the family. -We want to love the real world, not the virtual world.
Morning routines	- A day well-begun is half done. - We want hardworking, self-sufficient children who jump-start each day with vigor and zeal. - "Early to bed and early to rise helps a man grow healthy, wealthy, and wise."

THE KFP FINALIZER™

STEP THREE: Craft a process name out of the area of life. Consider either a straightforward name, a punchy name, or clever name, whatever fits your family best.[26]

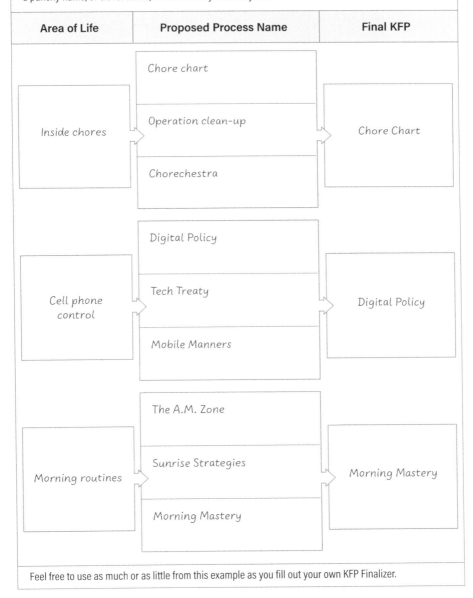

Area of Life	Proposed Process Name	Final KFP
Inside chores	Chore chart / Operation clean-up / Chorechestra	Chore Chart
Cell phone control	Digital Policy / Tech Treaty / Mobile Manners	Digital Policy
Morning routines	The A.M. Zone / Sunrise Strategies / Morning Mastery	Morning Mastery

Feel free to use as much or as little from this example as you fill out your own KFP Finalizer.

---

26 I have found Chat GPT to be helpful in coming up with creative names.

THE KFP FINALIZER™

STEP ONE: List those areas of life that are both (a) recurring and (b) benefit from guidelines, rules, or routines.

STEP TWO: Pick the three to five areas of life above that make the biggest impact on your long-term family goals. Write down what makes these areas so important.

Area of Life	Why this area has significant impact on your long-term family goals

THE KFP FINALIZER™

STEP THREE: Craft a process name out of the area of life. Consider either a straightforward name, a punchy name, or clever name, whatever fits your family best.

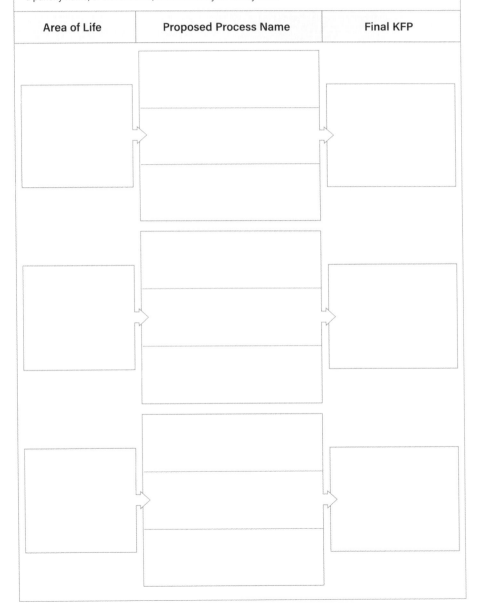

Area of Life	Proposed Process Name	Final KFP

Processes

While I have not taught elementary school, I have coached numerous little league baseball teams. At the beginning of every season, a handful of dads would pull me aside and say, "Hey, look coach, my Jimmy is really a pitcher. He's going through a little slump right now. He just wasn't himself in tryouts. But he's got a big future as a pitcher, so maybe you can rethink your positioning on the field."

And here is another even more significant example. Because my wife and I have a ton of kids, we have to listen to parents explain all the time why they stopped having kids. "My Johnny was so strong-willed. You have no idea . . ." "My Susie required so much attention as a baby that it nearly killed me. No discipline would work. People just don't understand what I went through." Well, what these parents don't understand (most of them, though I am sure there are exceptions) is that their child is not nearly as unique as they think. And I assure you that my wife and I did not just hit the jackpot fifteen times in a row with docile children.

In business, I have seen a dire need for executives to believe that their business is "totally unique" and that standard processes and professional coaching just don't work in their "niche industry." Likewise, families tend to do the same thing.

My advice is this: don't fall for it. Maybe you really do have a unique situation (families with a disabled child come to mind—God bless them). But the vast majority of families reading this book can apply these principles, just as most companies can apply basic business principles. Do not do your family the disservice of buying into the narrative that you are "so unique" that these principles do not apply to you. There is a place in the world to focus on uniqueness, but defining processes is probably not it. Even Albert Einstein had to be taught to read and make up his bed. In fact, as Einstein himself tells it, his early childhood accomplishments were nothing to brag about. He was slow to speak, and "my parents were so worried that they consulted a doctor," he reported. Little Albert only really began to bloom as a teenager.[27] So you

---

27 Isaacson, Walter. *American Sketches: Great Leaders, Creative Thinkers, and Heroes of a Hurricane.* New York, NY: Simon & Schuster, 2010, p. 128-130.

think you may have the next Einstein? How better could you serve him as a child than to teach him to put away his toys after playing with them, so he won't get tripped up by bad habits when he grows up to change the world?

CHORE CHARTS

One of our KFPs is a chore chart. The more kids you have, the more you need a chore chart. My family actually uses two chore charts, one for inside chores and one for outside chores. But this only happened because of a hard-learned lesson in my professional life.

In my business, I learned the beauty of managing processes through large whiteboards hanging on the wall. One day, I had a Master Blackbelt in Six Sigma consulting our executive team on our "Multimedia Production Process."

He asked us, "Do you folks understand this process?" "Sure we do," we all said. "Wow! That's impressive," he responded. He then gave each of us a piece of paper and pen. "Write down the steps in the process, one by one, on your own. Go." We all sort of looked around the room like unprepared high schoolers just handed a pop quiz. As the leader, I felt like an idiot, because I knew what was about to happen. After about five minutes, he collected the papers and read each one. The differences were staggering. They didn't even sound like the same process. Out of the six executives in the room, no two even had fifty percent of the steps overlapping. It was as if we each worked in a different business, speaking different languages. It was the corporate version of the Tower of Babel. All I could do was rub my forehead, thinking to myself, "What kind of leader am I?" The consultant let the silence hang in the air. He eventually followed up with a question. "So, I ask you again: do you folks understand this process?" We went around the room, one at a time, and said "No." It was a powerful moment for me.

About six hours later, we had a huge 60" x 48" whiteboard hanging in the hallway entitled "The Multimedia Production Process." It was a beautiful grid design with every essential task running down the left side and key dates running along the top. It was color-coded. It had responsible parties listed at different stages. We even had a picture of a rocket ship blasting off at the end of the production process when the product was "ready to launch." It was beautiful. It was elegant. It changed our business life.

Daily Chores

SUNDAY	MONDAY	TUESDAY	WEDNESDAY
Peter	Jude	David	Imelda
Jude	Peter	Imelda	David
Paul	Teresa	Jude A.M. Paul P.M.	Annie
Teresa	Paul	Annie	Luke/ Thomas
Imelda	David	Peter	Paul

Inside

THURSDAY	FRIDAY	SATURDAY	
Annie	Teresa	Paul	Dishes
Jude A.M. Paul P.M.	Paul	Teresa	Countertops
Imelda	Peter	Jude	Kitchen / Dining Room Floors
David	Jude	Peter	Rest of Downstairs
Jude	Luke/ Thomas	Imelda	Bonus Room Pick Up / Vacuum

At home, I realized getting the household chores done was not that different. Just like my executives, each person in my family (my wife, the high-schoolers, the middle school kids, and even the little guys just old enough to help with little tasks) all had a different expectation every single night. No wonder we had so much conflict with chores! Each night, my wife and I (usually my wife) would have to assign tasks to three or four kids. From their standpoint, the tasks were always changing, and they didn't know when they would get slammed with chores or have the luxury of an evening off.

And so, I sat with my wife and "mapped out" the essential chores. We grouped them in easy-to-understand language such as *Dishes*, *Countertops*, *Floors*, and *Rest of Downstairs*. We created a grid on a chalkboard so that it is easy to edit. You can see what it looks like on the next page.

Now, I'm not saying this chart magically solved all our chore conflicts and is guaranteed to do the same for you. But I will tell you that once we added this as a KFP, we haven't stopped. And our house sure is a lot quieter and more orderly because of it.

THE FAMILY DIGITAL POLICY

Another KFP in my house is the Family Digital Policy. It is an inescapable reality that smartphones, iPads, gaming systems, and computers are destroying our humanity. If you only have little kids, this section might be a few years early. But your time will come.

The statistics of how much screen time young children are consuming is staggering. The purpose of this book, however, is not to convince you that too much screen time with a smartphone is bad for your kid. You know that, even if you don't know how bad.[28]

Screen time, especially with smartphones, can be addictive because it affects dopamine levels in the brain. When we engage with screens, activities like social media, gaming, or receiving notifications trigger dopamine release, creating a pleasurable feeling. This process reinforces the behavior, making

---

28 Screen time has been linked to increased risk of obesity, poor sleep, poor physical health, increased risk of anxiety, depression, and other mental health issues, decreased social and cognitive development. "Screen Time Impact on Children Statistics 2023: Key Insights And Trends," GITNUX, October 15, 2023, https://blog.gitnux.com/screen-time-impact-on-children-statistics/.

THE DIGITAL POLICY BUILDER™

CURRENT STATE

What Works List any existing policies, formal or informal, that work well.	What Doesn't Work List any existing policies, formal or informal, that do not work well.
- Set a timer at the beginning of screen time. - Screen time is used as a reward for good behavior.	- Undefined video game and TV time limit. - Unclear parameters of appropriate shows to watch with the entire family.

FUTURE STATE

PURPOSE/OBJECTIVES
Craft a statement explaining why this is so important for the family and the individuals.

We need to protect our family from potentially harmful material, give them guard rails to make good digital choices for themselves, and have clear guidelines so the entire family knows what is and is not allowed.

When

Time of Day	Screen Time	Driving	Other
- Weekdays after school. - Specific times on weekends.	- 45 mins on week-days. - 2 hours on typical days on weekend.	- Phones are only used by passengers. - Travel with phones in case of emergency.	- No screens allowed during family meal times.

Who / Where

Who		Where	
Allowed	Not Allowed	Allowed	Not Allowed
- Approved friends and family. - Teachers and coaches.	- Strangers. - Unapproved friends.	- Common family areas in house. - In public where appropriate.	- Bedrooms. - Near dinner table during meals.

What

Permitted Content	Prohibited Content
- Dude Perfect. - Bluey and Kid Crew. - Sports games.	- Fortnite and similar video games. - Unapproved TV shows / YouTube content.

THE DIGITAL POLICY BUILDER™

CURRENT STATE

What Works List any existing policies, formal or informal, that work well.	What Doesn't Work List any existing policies, formal or informal, that do not work well.

FUTURE STATE

PURPOSE/OBJECTIVES
Craft a statement explaining why this is so important for the family and the individuals.

When

Time of Day	Screen Time	Driving	Other

Who		Where	
Allowed	Not Allowed	Allowed	Not Allowed

What

Permitted Content	Prohibited Content

us want to use devices more frequently. Over time, this constant stimulation and reward cycle can lead to compulsive device use and potential addiction. Excessive screen time has been linked to various negative effects on mental health, such as increased anxiety, depression, and sleep disturbances.[29]

It's easy to see why some form of smartphone policy is an obvious Key Family Process. What is your smartphone or gaming or computer family policy? The Digital Policy Builder™ has a generic name to cover all electronic devices. You may, however, want to craft separate smartphone, gaming, and computer policies. As always, feel free to use as much or as little that applies to your family from the example provided.

CONCLUSION

Congratulations! You've now developed a series of systems that will be an integral part of your Well-Ordered Family. The quote I've repeated several times, "A bad system beats a good person," no longer applies to you or your family.

Take a moment to celebrate. You've taken an important step in your Family Management System toward a well-ordered family. It's a big accomplishment.

But remember step four in the Deming method, quality control. It's an action as important as creating the system itself, the step that kept all those decades of Toyotas running, and running, and running . . .

You have to take measures to keep yourself and your family accountable. That's not a metaphor, either! Literally take measures. Let's discuss how to do that.

---

29 Perhaps the greatest danger is exposure to pornography and sexually explicit media, but this goes beyond the scope of this book.

PART-4

METRICS

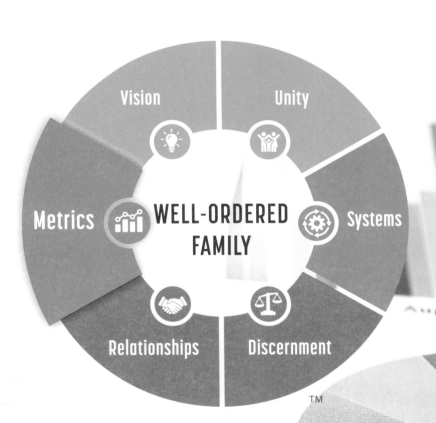

Vision

Unity

Metrics

WELL-ORDERED
FAMILY

Systems

Relationships

Discernment

TM

"In God we trust, all others must bring data."

–W. EDWARDS DEMING

CHAPTER

9

MEASURABLES

My son just couldn't get his basketball shot right. There was something off about his technique, particularly his elbow placement. After telling him repeatedly, "Keep your elbow down rather than flaring it out," I realized he couldn't *feel* what I was seeing.

In order to feel it, he needed to measure it. He needed to put some quantifiable standard on his elbow. So, I asked him to imagine a clock face and measure his shooting elbow's position. "Your goal is to get your elbow at six o'clock," I told him. From there, after each shot, I asked, "Where was it?" He answered four o'clock numerous times. Eventually, he got it to five o'clock. Many times, I disagreed with his assessment but kept my mouth shut. The point was *not* for him to get the measurement right but to become aware of measurement as a standard of performance. Eventually, he got it down around six o'clock. A huge success.

I had spent the past several weeks trying to get him to keep his elbow down, with no improvement. But when I introduced measurement into the equation, we reached our goal in less than three minutes.

The power of measurement.

YOU CAN MEASURE ANYTHING

Every single thing in the world can be measured, even the intangibles, albeit imperfectly. Successful athletes, chefs, scientists, CFOs, and marketers recognize the significance of measuring what matters. Athletes track performance metrics for skill improvement, chefs measure ingredients for consistency, scientists rely on precise measurements for accurate conclusions, CFOs assess financial data for strategic decisions, and marketers use metrics to optimize campaigns and understand consumers. Measuring what matters empowers excellence and continual improvement across the board.

CAN YOU MEASURE LOVE?

Love, often considered the most elusive intangible, is commonly perceived as immeasurable—devoid of weight, dimensions, and quantifiable metrics. However, with a touch of creativity, flexibility, and subjectivity, we can find ways to measure some of its important aspects.

Take spousal love. First, we need to consider different facets of spousal love. The popular book by Gary Chapman, *The Five Love Languages*,[30] uses these categories: gifts, physical touch, quality time, acts of service, and words of affirmation. These are five very different ways to express and perceive love. A diamond ring, a hug, watching a movie together, taking out the garbage, and paying a compliment are all very different things, but each can be an expression of love. You and your spouse must choose particular ways in which love is displayed in your life.[31] With careful thought and communication, you can come up with ways to measure any love language. Perhaps you exchange a small monthly gift or enjoy a date night once a week. Maybe you make sure to sit close to your spouse when watching TV, knock out a few extra items on the honey-do list, or make sure to say something complimentary to your spouse each day.

---

30 Chapman, Gary. *The 5 Love Languages: The Secret to Love that Lasts*. Northfield Publishing, 2015.

31 In saying this, I do not imply that love, or more properly stated as charity, is a subjective or relativistic reality. There are many objective standards to love that personal preference can never change. Love, properly understood, is desiring the true good for another human being, and it is certainly not desiring to merely meet the desires of another human being. Nonetheless, married couples have their particularities. Each family is constituted differently. And thus, particular manifestations of love appear in different forms.

These quantifiable measures often serve as decent, albeit imperfect, representations of the efforts made to express love in a spousal relationship. They are by no means the only components of love, just the signs we can measure. As with all measurements, they are not the whole truth, but they are useful.

CAN SIN AND VIRTUE BE MEASURED?

> "If you cannot measure it, you cannot improve it."
>
> *—Lord Kelvin*

Both sin and virtue, often deemed intangible, have measurable aspects. An examination of conscience allows us to track and gauge the frequency of our faults and failings. To make this a reality, just set an alarm on your phone for 3:00 p.m. every day and label it "Self-Reflection."

Drawing inspiration from the *Spiritual Exercises of Ignatius of Loyola*,[32] an age-old practice encourages writing down the vices we aim to overcome. Make a list, and then periodically throughout the day, examine your conscience on these specific issues. If the vice was present, mark it down on the list. It's not perfect or precise, but it does help measurement become a habit, which is essential for growth. It's not unlike my son measuring the placement of his elbow when shooting a basketball. And I would bet a lot of money that, just like I didn't care so much how accurate my son's assessment was, God cares less about the accuracy of my measurement than He cares about the fact that I *am* measuring and remeasuring. The act of measurement itself brings the matter to my consciousness, where my will can act on it.

Of course, if you are a Protestant, you may want to think of vices as shortcomings, ways you fall short of walking within the will of the Lord. If you are of some other faith or not religious, perhaps think of them as signs you are not comporting yourself with the natural law scribed within your being.

No matter what you call the bad stuff, measure it!

---

32 Ignatius. *The Spiritual Exercises of Saint Ignatius*. Charlotte, NC: TAN Classics, 2010.

It's always bothered me that the spiritual life is seen as immeasurable while health and fitness and finances are seen as measurable. A little scenario might prove my point.

Imagine I went to a fitness instructor and said, "If you help me get six-pack abs in the next six months, I'll give you $50,000." What would he do? He would measure everything: my calories in, calories out, my macro nutrients, my sleep cycles, maybe even insulin level, the progression in cardio and strength. He would give me a detailed plan for working out, for recovery, and injury prevention. The metrics would be awesome.

Now, imagine I went to a business consultant and said, "If you improve my cash flow over the next six months by five percent, I will give you $50,000." He would also measure everything: accounts payable and accounts receivable, inventory turns, profit margins on upcoming product releases, bloated payroll and other expenses, and so on.

But if I go to someone and ask for spiritual direction (as I have often done), I usually get simple advice like, "Pray for twenty minutes a day and make sure to date your wife." What I want is a detailed plan to obtain virtue, some way to track and measure progress and failure. Granted, the spiritual life is different by nature. But I think that a far greater metrics-based spiritual program might help me do better in the unmeasurable aspects of spiritual growth.

Activities like prayer, fasting, conquering vice, spiritual reading, works of mercy and charity, and, for a Catholic at least, regular confession can be measured and tracked on a spiritual scorecard. Even abstract principles like "surrender to divine providence" can be placed on a spectrum where we personally assess and slide the scale between *better* and *worse*. Regularly reviewing our perception and tracking progress nurtures spiritual growth and transformation.

In essence, both sin and virtue can be measured in our daily lives. There's nothing profound or impossible about doing so. By developing this habit of measurement, we gain valuable insights into our spiritual progress and cultivate a deeper understanding of our relationships with God and others. Embracing the notion that we can measure both our faults and acts of goodness empowers us to embark on a purposeful journey toward spiritual development and fulfillment.

GOAL SETTING

Three days ago, I read in a local paper (yes, a real physical newspaper) that a young husband and father ran a 50-mile ultramarathon around Charlotte, North Carolina, and stopped and prayed at many churches on his route. It was like an ultra-prayer-athon. Pretty cool.

Ashley was driving as I read this story to her from the passenger seat. When I was done, she simply said, "Don't even think about it, Conor."

"What do you mean?" I innocently asked.

"I know exactly what's going on in your head. But every time you start running you get hurt. And that kid is probably twenty-something. You aren't. So put it out of your mind."

Hmm. Truth be told, she was right.

I'm a man with a pulse, aren't I? Of course I was thinking about that!

I could do it, too. I still got it. I can train. At that point, I'm already hearing the intro to *Eye of the Tiger* in my head.

My wife knows me so well. She recognizes that I would start strong, go too hard, get injured, and end up putting on an extra ten pounds for my trouble.

We men watch documentaries on climbing Mount Everest, or about guys who run miles through the Sahara Desert and think, "yeah, with the proper training, that could be me. Why not?"

And then we tweak a muscle in our backs pulling the trash bag out of the trashcan.

Yet these outliers, those masters of human accomplishment, really do have something to teach those of us living normal lives. Whether you are running an ultramarathon or simply helping your high schooler improve his GPA, sustained success requires goal setting.

WHEN THE GOAL CHANGES

My oldest was a highly competitive baseball player. He was a switch-hitting catcher. Not a bad combo. He was also on his way to being competitive in CrossFit. He was packing on a lot of muscle. But the time had come for him to decide whether or not he would pursue baseball in college. It was a tough decision for someone who had worked so hard for many years.

I remember the conversation. We were lifting weights together in the garage. He told me about his deliberation, his back-and-forth thoughts. And then he asked me a really tough question.

"Dad, what is the likelihood that I could become a major league player?"

Now, you might think this has an easy answer. But here was a young man on the cusp of manhood. He was about to step into reality in a way that little boys do not need to.

I considered carefully, then told him the unvarnished truth.

"Son, you have displayed remarkable discipline. And I'm very proud of you. You've totally risen to the top of your team and league. But in reality, there isn't any top level competition around here. The bar has been comparatively low. The chances of your becoming a major league player are not good, but also not impossible. Besides, I want you to have a well-rounded life and experience the joy of many different interests. But the choice is yours."

Ultimately, he decided to stop playing baseball and take up umpiring.

When he made that decision, my advice to him was this. "Son, I respect your decision. But now I want you to decide what excellence means for you in being an umpire. How do you become a tier one umpire? How do you choose a goal in umpiring? How do you set milestones along the way?"

After consideration, he set a goal to become a Division I college umpire while still *in* college.

It was lofty. It was wildly ambitious. I wasn't sure it was even possible. Neither was he.

In order to accomplish this seemingly impossible goal, he took every Little League game he could find. He networked with the other umpires. He learned that there are numerous certifications one can acquire. He earned them.

He went to umpire training camps.

He networked with even more experienced umps.

Eventually, he got a break and was asked to umpire a varsity high school game while still in high school! Some of the players were older than he was. Then, as a freshman in college, he got his first break and began to umpire recreational college games.

He even found a part-time job working for an umpire association, doing some basic social media marketing. He networked so much that a major league umpire (one who had umped multiple World Series) one day called him on the phone! That's right. Aiden got a call from a World Series umpire because he had heard so much about this young kid giving umpiring his all.

Aiden made it a goal to buy the best equipment, the best uniform, to show up to games in a sports coat and socialize with the other umpires in a polished manner. He came across as a young professional, not just as a guy making a couple of bucks on the side.

Aiden stood out. Big time.

Eventually, he made his way to Division III games, and then Division II. And one day, he finally got the call to umpire a Division I college game. He was even chosen as an alternate for the local minor league team. At the time, he was a junior in College. He was told that he was the youngest Division I umpire in the nation.

My son, Aiden Gallagher, reached his goal.

Why was this so important for him? To get a good hourly rate as a college umpire? No. He had a goal in his mind and heart, one that stretched years ahead of the present. It was this goal that drove his everyday decisions.

GOALS DRIVE EVERYTHING

I enjoy looking at human history through the lens of goal setting. Often, we see the incredible accomplishments of historical figures, but fail to notice they usually had a remarkably refined and lofty goal that they painstakingly, sometimes obsessively, worked toward. Perhaps the genius is more in framing superior goals and goal management than the accomplishment itself.

Consider just a few examples of goal setting in the history of corporate America, all of which have provided us with our comfortable standards of living:

Henry Ford:
- *Goal:* Revolutionize the automobile industry, for the first time making cars affordable for the masses.
- *Achievement:* Developed efficient manufacturing processes, created the Model T, and implemented the assembly line, transforming automobile production.

Steve Jobs:
- *Goal:* Create pioneering, elegant, and user-friendly technology products.
- *Achievement:* Cofounded Apple Inc., producing groundbreaking devices like the iPhone, iPad, and Macintosh computers, redefining technology interaction.

Elon Musk:
- *Goal:* Advance sustainable energy and space exploration.
- *Achievement:* Founded Tesla, SpaceX, and SolarCity, revolutionizing transportation and pushing the boundaries of space exploration. Also revolutionized e-commerce as part of the PayPal founding team to jumpstart his entrepreneurial career.

Andrew Carnegie:
- *Goal:* Become one of the wealthiest men and dedicate wealth to philanthropy.
- *Achievement:* Established Carnegie Steel Company, becoming the world's largest and most profitable steel company. Supported education, libraries, and charitable causes.

Thomas Edison:
- *Goal:* Invent and innovate to improve people's lives.
- *Achievement:* Held over a thousand patents, inventing the phonograph, motion picture camera, and practical electric light bulb, revolutionizing various industries.

Jeff Bezos:
- *Goal:* Revolutionize e-commerce and create the world's largest online marketplace.
- *Achievement:* Founded Amazon.com, starting as an online bookstore and expanding into a multinational conglomerate offering a wide product selection and convenient shopping experiences.

Goal setting is perhaps the most impressive in the realm of physical feats. There, the goal seems to expand reality itself, or at least what humans imagined reality to be. Here are a few examples in which human capacity was stretched to new limits to meet the lofty goal:

Roger Bannister:
- *Goal:* Break the four-minute mile barrier, generally believed to be physiologically impossible until 1954.[33]
- *Achievement:* On May 6, 1954, he ran a mile in 3 minutes and 59.4 seconds, becoming the first to achieve this feat. His success inspired athletes worldwide to push their limits.

Edmund Hillary and Tenzing Norgay:
- *Goal:* Reach the summit of Mount Everest, at 29,032 feet above sea level, the world's highest peak.
- *Achievement:* On May 29, 1953, they became the first confirmed climbers to reach the summit. Their achievement marked a significant milestone in mountaineering history.

Usain Bolt:
- *Goal:* Break records and dominate world-wide sprinting events.
- *Achievement:* He set numerous world records in the 100 meters, 200 meters, and 4x100 meters relay, establishing himself as the fastest man in the world.

---

33 https://www.britannica.com/biography/Roger-Bannister.

S.M.A.R.T. FAMILY GOALS

Use the acronym, S.M.A.R.T. (Specific, Measurable, Achievable, Relevant, Time-bound) to define criteria to focus your goal and improve your chance of success.

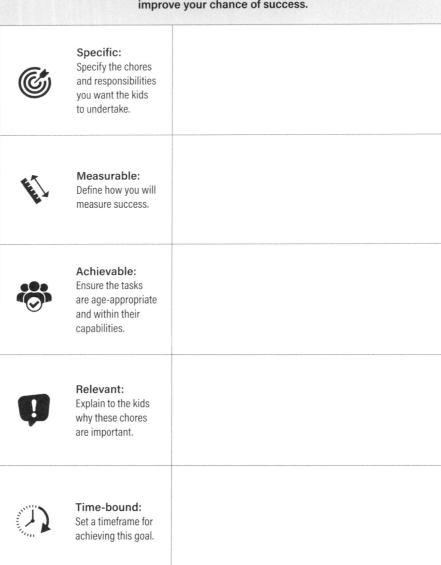

Specific: Specify the chores and responsibilities you want the kids to undertake.	
Measurable: Define how you will measure success.	
Achievable: Ensure the tasks are age-appropriate and within their capabilities.	
Relevant: Explain to the kids why these chores are important.	
Time-bound: Set a timeframe for achieving this goal.	

Alex Honnold:
- *Goal:* Free solo climb El Capitan in Yosemite National Park.
- *Achievement:* On June 3, 2017, he accomplished this extraordinary feat without any ropes or safety equipment, showcasing exceptional physical strength and mental focus.

Diana Nyad:
- *Goal:* Swim from Cuba to Florida without a shark cage.
- *Achievement:* On September 2, 2013, *at sixty-four years old,* she completed the 110-mile swim, becoming the first person to do so. Her journey demonstrated incredible endurance, determination, and belief in her abilities.

With countless examples of the power of goal setting all around us, it should be surprising that we so often neglect it in the most precious segment of our lives. We can use all the powerful tools associated with accomplishing magnificent feats. Raising a happy and virtuous family is the most magnificent feat of all.

Remember our definition: A goal is a *specific* and *measurable* objective or desired outcome with a set timeframe.

Next, let's talk about how to formulate goals that are *specific.*

S.M.A.R.T. FAMILY GOALS

We spoke before about S.M.A.R.T. goals when we set the Three-Year Household Goals for your Family Master Plan™. You might recall that the acronym S.M.A.R.T. stands for Specific, Measurable, Achievable, Relevant, and Time-Bound.

Understanding how to properly set goals is vital to your family's success. Without S.M.A.R.T. goals, you are setting your family up for frustration and failure. In this regard, keeping score of your own behavior is helpful in knowing whether you are attaining your goals.

In business, I have struggled with goal setting for years. Inevitably, our Quarterly Rocks (a term for must-accomplish, medium-term business goals) will initially be articulated as something like "Get the App going" or "Fix the Customer Service issue." But what does "going" mean? What does "fix" mean? These words lack specificity. And at the end of ninety days, it is all too common for the status report to be something like "Well, the App is basically done, but it is still in beta mode. But it's definitely going." See how squishy things get when goals are loosely defined?

It's no different in your family. If your goal is "improve finances," the husband might think things are worse because the debt number went up, but the wife might think things are better because she is wisely using a cash-based system and spending less on groceries each month. Both might be true. The problem is that the goal was badly phrased from the start.

Here's a more detailed example. What if your goal with teenagers was "do better in school"? There is plenty of wiggle room for this to be debated. And thus, we need S.M.A.R.T. Goals.

- **Specific:** The goal should be clear and well-defined. Instead of a vague goal like "I want to do better in school," a specific goal might be "I want to improve my math grades."
- **Measurable:** There should be a way to track and measure progress. For academic performance, this could involve setting a target grade or a specific grade point average (GPA) increase. For example, "I want to raise my math grade from a C to a B."
- **Achievable:** The goal should be realistic and attainable. It should stretch the individual but still be within reach. Setting an unrealistic goal, like jumping from a C to an A+, might not be achievable in one semester. A more attainable goal could be "I want to raise my math grade from a C to a B."
- **Relevant:** The goal should align with the individual's overall objectives and values. In the context of a teenager's academic performance, the goal should relate to his educational aspirations and future plans. For instance, it would be great if he could say, "Improving my math grade is relevant because I want to pursue a career in engineering." But it is a slippery slope to try to tie every course with a career. He might have to settle for "Getting a better math grade is relevant to being a responsible young man." And it is!
- **Time-Bound:** A deadline should be set for achieving the goal. Without a timeframe, it's easy to procrastinate. An example of a time-bound goal might be "I want to raise my math grade from a C to a B by the end of this semester."

With this S.M.A.R.T. goal in place, the teenager has a clear plan:

- **Specific:** He wants to improve his math grade.
- **Measurable:** He will track his progress based on his math grade.
- **Achievable:** Going from a C to a B is a realistic step.
- **Relevant:** It aligns with his career aspirations or performing his duties.
- **Time-Bound:** He has a clear deadline (the end of the semester).

And to underscore just how integral S.M.A.R.T. goals are to get your family on the right path, here's an example of a more shared goal that involves setting sub-goals for both you and your younger children.

Let's say the goal is "to improve the involvement of my little kids (ages four and six) in household chores to teach them responsibility and help with family tasks."

- **Specific:** Specify the chores and responsibilities you want the kids to undertake. For example, "I want my four-year-old to put all the shoes in the shoe basket every night and my six-year-old to assist in clearing the table after dinner."
- **Measurable:** Define how you will measure success. This could involve tracking the number of times they successfully complete their assigned chores each week. For instance, "Both kids should complete their chores at least three times a week without being told."
- **Achievable:** Ensure the tasks are age-appropriate and within their capabilities. Don't expect perfection, but rather aim for gradual improvement. The four-year-old probably won't get all the shoes in the shoe basket at first. But getting his own shoes in the shoe basket is a good start!
- **Relevant:** Explain to the kids why these chores are important. Emphasize how helping with household tasks contributes to the family's well-being and teaches them valuable life skills.
- **Time-Bound:** Set a timeframe for achieving this goal. For example, "Within the next month, I want both kids to consistently complete their assigned chores three times a week without being told."

To review: A goal is a *specific* and *measurable* objective or desired outcome with a set timeframe. S.M.A.R.T. goals are perfect for getting specific.

But what, you may ask, can I *measure* in family life? It feels like a crazy quilt of seemingly unquantifiable activity. Family life consists of countless tasks.

Housekeeping. Carpool driving. Paying bills. You name it. But, more importantly, family life consists of emotions and passions, of tears and laughter.

How am I supposed to measure the amount of joy in the Gallagher family? Every time my kids hit each other am I supposed to run to a big chalkboard and tick a deduction? Each time my wife gives me a little smile of affection am I supposed to say, "Hang on honey. I gotta track that in my app."

No, not like that. But even though you may think that the most important things in your life, such as love and anger and joy and sorrow, are *not* trackable, I'm here to tell you that they *are*. Imperfectly, of course. You note, in a way, the effects and not the cause.

But it can be done! And I'm going to show you how with The Family Scorecard™.

But first, let's consider that most measurable aspect of family life: *habits*.

CHAPTER

11

HABITS

Not too long ago, I was struggling with my health. Raising my kids and running my businesses had all but erased any personal priority of eating well and exercising. I didn't wake up one morning and start making terrible decisions about what I ate and how physically active I was (or wasn't). But incrementally, my personal habits put me in a near perilous position with Type 2 diabetes. I'll never forget reading how people diagnosed with Type 2 diabetes at my age had a fifty percent chance of having a stroke, heart attack, or amputation by age sixty-five. *Amputation?* For some reason, the thought of having a limb cut off rocked my world!

This caused me to completely reevaluate my eating and exercise habits. Thankfully, through an improved diet and regular physical activity, I was able to turn my personal health situation around and am in a much better place now.

But the only way I did that was by breaking down weight loss and exercise into weekly routines and daily habits.

I took the big goal of losing forty pounds and broke it down into smaller pieces. I tracked calories and wrote down my weight every single day.

I might've lost a few pounds through sheer willpower and common sense in the weeks after first reading about the possibility of future amputation, but there's no way I would've achieved any sustainable results without changing my habits. The most important aspect of this process for me wasn't cutting out sugar. It was *becoming accountable* for everything I ate by writing it down. I didn't always eat perfectly. But I was always accountable for what I ate because I decided to track it. And, so far, I still retain both arms and legs and hope to keep them attached for the rest of my life!

THE FAMILY HABIT TRACKER™

I can't overemphasize the importance of forming good habits. It was Aristotle who defined a virtue as a habit inclined toward the good (in part). Likewise, he defined vice as a habit inclined toward evil.

Each quarter, it would be great if your family set in motion a few new habits. They can be very simple.

- Say please and thank you
- Everyone clears their own dishes from the table
- Hang out together outside instead of in front of the TV
- Make up your bed
- Give up rolling your eyes

The list could go on and on. If you made a simple list of family habits to work on, placed it on the refrigerator, and looked at it on occasion, you might experience extraordinary results.

How long does it take to form a habit? The notion of it taking twenty-one days seems to be a myth, though it is a good start for considering the matter. The psychological debate on this point can be fierce,[34] but some facts are clear. First, it takes time to break an old habit, which is different than forming a new habit. Second, it takes longer for a habit to become permanent. Third, habits come in all shapes and sizes, so some areas of life are harder to form habits in than others. The range provided by expert studies is so big (18–254 days) that it isn't even helpful to consider. I think it's most convenient to return to use

---

[34] Solis-Moreira, Jocelyn. "How Long Does It Really Take to Form a Habit?" Scientific American, January 30, 2024. https://www.scientificamerican.com/article/how-long-does-it-really-take-to-form-a-habit/.

a three-month framework. Given that the world with its seasons and everything in it rotates around ninety-day cycles, why not spend the quarter forming a new habit? Ninety days will get you well on your way to making a habit permanent.

Use The Family Habit Tracker™ (see example on page 168) to track your progress.

ROCKS

One of the most influential modern books ever written is *The 7 Habits of Highly Effective People* by Stephen R. Covey.[35] *7 Habits* has become part of American parlance. Many people feel they know the book but have never actually read it. I highly recommend you do.

Covey famously presents the parable-like analogy of a glass jar, rocks, pebbles, sand, and water. If you put anything in the glass first other than the rocks, you run out of space for everything. Rocks must go in first. Then, the pebbles next, which fill the big space between the rocks. Next, the sand pours in between the rocks and pebbles. Finally, the water slips into every crack and crevice. It's just like packing a suitcase: you have to put the big stuff in first.

EOS and other business systems have brilliantly applied Covey's concept of "rocks" to mean quarterly goals. These are the most important priorities on a ninety-day basis. And so, you now have tens of thousands of managers saying, "Did you get your rocks done?" and we all know they are referring to quarterly goals.

At my business, reviewing and choosing rocks has become the heart and soul of the business rhythm. Everyone on the management team has rocks. On a good quarter, we hit 85 percent of the rocks. On a bad quarter, we might only hit 50 percent. To be frank, we've never hit 100 percent. Perhaps we are too aspirational; perhaps 80–90 percent is just right.

You can picture a rock. Rocks can be valuable ore, and they can also be diamonds. The term "rock" is also beneficial because we overuse the words

---

35 Covey, Stephen R. *The 7 Habits of Highly Effective People: 30th Anniversary Edition*. New York, NY: Simon & Schuster, 2020.

"goal" or "objective" or "priority." There are long-term goals, annual priorities, and so on. Rock, in this parlance, means 90 days. When we say "rock," it specifically indicates a quarterly goal. It's a nice way to distinguish.

When it comes to Family Rocks, think about those unfinished projects or unresolved issues that gnaw at you. It's what I find myself pondering when I'm sitting in traffic at a red light. A rock is not something you can knock out in an hour. A Family Rock is typically an issue that's going to need a multi-step process to resolve.

- Fix the gutter issue near the garage
- Plan the next summer vacation
- Purchase a family car
- Decide where to give a family Christmas donation
- Get the kids to the dentist
- Plan a wedding/anniversary celebration/birthday party
- Organize a community service project
- Lose ten pounds (Dad)
- Set a family budget

Completing these Family Rocks typically requires a process that involves at least three steps.

1. Investigation
2. Communication
3. Execution

Let's use that sagging, leaky garage gutter listed above as an example. First, you have to figure out exactly what the issue is. Is it a simple clog or has the sheet metal come loose? This can take some serious time and effort to find out. Once you know exactly what the problem is and how to fix it, then you have to figure out what materials you need. And you need to know who is going to do the repair work and schedule it. Finally, the job has to get done and done right so it won't be a perpetual problem that plagues you for longer than it already has.

For increased clarity and to avoid confusion, put *one person in your family* in charge of each Family Rock. That provides accountability and a sense of shared responsibility that's important for any group, especially a family. And don't be afraid to set a deadline that's before the end of the quarter. Some Family Rocks might need to be resolved in less than ninety days. And some family members might need a little deadline pressure to get things moving.

Family Rocks are designed to be tracked on The Family Scorecard. So let's get to the heart of measuring and accountability for the Well-Ordered Family!

THE FAMILY HABIT TRACKER™

	1	2	3	4	5	6	7	8	9	10	11	12
Clear dishes	X			X	X	X	X	X	X	X	X	X
Outside time						X			X			X
Make up bed	X				X			X			X	

THE FAMILY HABIT TRACKER™

JANUARY	FEBUARY	MARCH
APRIL	MAY	JUNE
JULY	AUGUST	SEPTEMBER
OCTOBER	NOVEMBER	DECEMBER

13	14	15	16	17	18	19	20	21	22	23	24	25	26	27	28	29	30	31
		X	X	X	X			X	X	X	X			X				
X									X		X				X	X	X	X
		X					X						X	X		X	X	

"What gets measured gets managed."

–PETER DRUCKER

CHAPTER

12

MEASURING FAMILY LIFE

Let the disclaimers begin! Your family is not a sports team, an assembly line of units of production, or a test subject in a lab. They are valuable individuals whose worth far surpasses any quantifiable metric. But natural law still prevails. Your spouse and children are human beings that need accountability.

We cannot "run" our families with the same level of accountability that we run a business. Nonetheless, the use of measurement tools in family life is underappreciated.

In this chapter, I will help you figure out what you want to measure. Then, I will show you how to create your own Family Scorecard. In the next chapter, we will discuss how to keep the family accountable for the scores on The Family Scorecard™ without alienating, shaming, or micromanaging. The Family Scorecard™ is just that, a running tally. It's not a final pronouncement on any family member's virtue or shame, but a pragmatic tool to gauge progress.

THE FAMILY SCORECARD™

What area does your family need to improve the most? In my mind, that can be a daunting question. Breaking that thought down into smaller pieces helps me to get going in the right direction. For example, let's say you want to improve the family finances (who doesn't?). Financial improvement is a tough nut to crack—perhaps the toughest—because it is so broad and touches on so many areas.

But if I break down the idea of financial improvement to a much smaller concept, like saving twenty dollars a week on groceries or going out to eat one less time per month, it feels much less intimidating and much more doable. And when you actually write this down and track the results, you can literally see your family make progress. In my experience, the *measuring* is when the real improvement begins!

Here are some other examples of measurables for your family:

- **Academics:** Measuring GPAs as a tangible indicator of scholastic progress. Additionally, especially in homeschooling settings, tracking completed schoolwork becomes essential, with a measure of how many reminders are needed.
- **Interior Life:** Following our commitment to regular church services, daily prayer time, and other activities that reflect our spiritual dedication. (Since I am Catholic, confession and adoration come to mind for me.)
- **Marriage:** Evaluating how much quality time we get with our spouse might include tracking the number of date nights, the times we pray together, and successful adherence to Weekly Marriage Check-Ins.
- **Fitness and Nutrition:** These are vital components of well-being, and we can set measurable goals for ourselves. For instance, aiming to work out three times a week for both Mom and Dad, and limiting indulgence in desserts to twice per week, provides concrete objectives to pursue.
- **Screen Time:** To maintain a healthy digital balance, we can measure screen time, ensuring it remains within a designated number of hours per week.
- **Household Chores:** This is easy to measure. We can utilize that simple chore chart we discussed in chapter 6, "Systemic Excellence," and keep track of how often Mom and Dad have to remind kids to perform their chores.

THE FAMILY SCORECARD GENERATOR™

BRAINSTORM
- Think of areas to improve for your family.
- Add your own at the bottom.
- Rank the current priority level.
- This exercise is relative. Rank in relation to each other.
  Try not to have more than seven #3s. Which is most pressing
  right now?

DIRECTIONS
Circle 1, 2, 3, or N/A to indicate current priority level.
1: Unimportant or doesn't need extra focus right now
2: Moderately important and could use more focus
3: Needs immediate improvement
N/A: Doesn't currently apply

Area to Improve	Ranking			
Spending quality time together	1	2	3	N/A
Completing inside chores	1	2	3	N/A
Completing outside chores	1	2	3	N/A
Eating together as a family	1	2	3	N/A
Healthy eating habits	1	2	3	N/A
Physical fitness for Mom and Dad	1	2	3	N/A
Household budgeting and financial planning	1	2	3	N/A
Academic performance, including study habits, homework completion, and the resulting grades	1	2	3	N/A
Reading routine for the kids	1	2	3	N/A
Holding family meetings	1	2	3	N/A
Monitoring technology use and screen time	1	2	3	N/A
Family prayer routine	1	2	3	N/A

THE FAMILY SCORECARD GENERATOR™		
SPECIFY & DESCRIBE In the space below, write down no more than seven areas to improve, preferably from the list of items ranked 3 above. Now describe the current state. Why is it an area that needs improvement? Try to put in any quantifiable items that come to mind. If you can look up the numbers, go do it.		**ENVISION** Envision what the future state could be like for each of these areas. Make sure this is realistic and achievable.
Area to Improve	**Describe the Current State**	**Envision a Future State**
Family Meals	1–2 times on a good week	At least 3 per week
High Schooler's Grades	2.2 overall GPA. Being lazy	Gets overall GPA up to 3.0
Reading Routine for the Kids	Only reading for school, not pleasure	Finish one non-school book this quarter

Use The Family Scorecard Generator™ above to help you decipher what metrics are most important for your family. Brainstorm and then specify, describe, and envision.

Please understand I don't mean to say making significant changes in your family life is easy. I am saying that it is possible. And I know it's much more likely to happen if you set yourself up to succeed by measuring your progress and keeping accounts. Think of The Family Scorecard™ as a health tracker for the soul of your family. You've already identified the most important areas you want to improve, clearly reported the current state of those issues, and envisioned a better future. Now it's critical to come up with realistic goals and ways to tick off progress in that direction.

Want your family to eat dinner together more often? Set a goal and then track how many times it actually happens. The Family Scorecard Generator™ allows for clear communication of both the goal and the progress in that direction.

This is also where Family Rocks come in, those mid-term goals that are essential landmarks within a year. Track them here!

Write down your specific areas to improve, the goal you want to accomplish, and exactly how—and how often—you will measure progress in the blank version of The Family Scorecard™ provided.

THE FAMILY SCORECARD™				
Area To Improve	**Goal**	**Month 1**	**Month 2**	**Month 3**
Family Dinners	More than 10 per month	7	6	8
High Schooler's Grades	>C+ on tests & projects	Yes	No	Yes
Reading Routine for Kids	>50 pages per month	8	14	12

THE FAMILY ROCKS		
Rock	**Person Responsible**	**Due Date**
Fix Garage Leak	Dad	End of Nov.
Plan Summer Vacation	Oldest Daughter	End of Dec.
Buy New Car	Mom	End of Dec.

One note to keep in mind when it comes to frequency: I recommend keeping how often you measure progress as simple as possible. Use the tool to find measurements that reflect the overall story, not the day-to-day subplots. No one wants to be micromanaged or feel like they're always lagging behind.

THE FAMILY SCORECARD™				
Area To Improve	Goal	Month 1	Month 2	Month 3

THE FAMILY ROCKS			
Rock	Person Responsible	Due Date	Progress %

So what do you do once you have The Family Scorecard™ humming? How do you check and use your results?

Apply them to the airy heights of family vision and family unity—those are areas where you can earn your true black belt in family management!

You can share The Family Scorecard™ results at The Quarterly Family Meeting™, and from there, set aside separate time to discuss any specifics. At The Annual Family Council™, you'll have time to take a larger look at The Family Scorecard™, evaluate your progress, and make decisions on how to make it better for your family moving forward.

CONCLUSION

Metrics are the best way to find simple solutions to problems that can seem unsolvable. Whether it's a business, personal, or family issue, tracking progress by measuring results helps us to let go of emotional attachment and focus on making the transition from an issue that's a problem in the present to a situation with improved outcomes in the near future. Setting S.M.A.R.T. goals and keeping your family accountable with The Family Scorecard™ will create a system of clear communication to help everyone rally around making the progress necessary to achieve those goals.

Systems. Metrics. With a thoughtful method and solid metrics you can build a family dynamic that will satisfy even W. Edward Deming, should his ghostly presence stop by for inspection!

Joking aside, I believe there's a portion fundamentally ingrained in us that is affirmed when we're a part of something bigger than ourselves. That's exactly the environment that metrics will help you create for your family. Seeing the numbers will clarify the reality for all involved.

But remember, the numbers point to the bigger picture, the higher meaning of family life.

Recall that you are the family's CEO, what I define as the resident visionary. The CEO's most important task is to work *on* the business, and not just in it. One of the best ways to do so is to develop a nuanced understanding of human nature so that you can better discern how to lead your family to a place where you can survive and thrive in your very own way.

PART-5

RELATIONSHIPS

Vision

Unity

Metrics

WELL-ORDERED FAMILY

Systems

Relationships

Discernment

TM

"All men by nature desire to know."

–ARISTOTLE

CHAPTER

13

HUMAN NATURE

Cesar Millan is the Dog Whisperer. His television show remains a huge hit. Viewers cannot get enough of seeing a dog run wild against its owner and then fall into complete submission within minutes or seconds once the Dog Whisperer walks in the room. Every episode seems nearly miraculous.

But it isn't. It is all common sense that is no longer common. Cesar's secret knowledge is simple. Your dog is a dog.

What does this mean? It means that in modern times, humans often treat dogs like humans—like human babies in particular. You've probably seen dogs being pushed around in strollers or dogs dragging their owner around on the leash. But the Dog Whisperer knows that a dog does not want a mommy or a daddy. It wants an alpha male. It does not want a family. It wants a pack. And thus, Cesar begins every episode with this burst of wisdom: "I rehabilitate dogs. I train people." He helps the dog become what it was born to be, and he teaches people how to let the dog be a dog.

Cesar understands the *nature* of a dog. A dog is not a cat, a horse, or a human. And nature dictates what will make a thing content. A fish without water will not be very happy. A dog without a pack will not be very happy. And a human without friendship will not be happy. Certain desires are hard-wired into our nature.

In Aesop's fable "The Scorpion and the Frog," one day, a scorpion asks a frog to carry it across a river. The frog is hesitant because it's afraid the scorpion will sting. This would, of course, mean instant death. The scorpion assures the frog that it won't. If it did, they would both drown. The frog finally allowed the scorpion to hop on board. Away they go across the river, the scorpion perched on the frog's back. Midway across, the scorpion stings the frog, dooming them both. The dying frog asks "why?" The scorpion replies, "I couldn't help it. It's in my nature." The moral of the story is that beings can't change their inherent nature, and it often leads to their own destruction.

There are horse whisperers who understand the nature of a horse so well that they communicate through body language in a way only a horse can understand. These horse whisperers can seemingly work magic and break a horse within minutes without "breaking it" at all.

To have a good relationship with a dog, you must understand what a dog needs. The same goes for a horse. The same goes for scorpions if you are a frog.

And the same goes for your family members. They are human. And to be human means something very particular.

GETTING BACK TO NATURE

A Well-Ordered Family is full of flourishing relationships between individual family members. Ancient Greek philosopher Aristotle has been considered an expert on the subject of human nature for about the last 2,400 years.

When your child is small, almost all your efforts as a parent go toward taking care of his body. But his soul is the thing that will last for eternity. We constantly undervalue the development of the soul in ways large and small.

As you can see, Aristotle breaks down the soul into thinking and non-thinking.

The thinking soul represents human rationality.

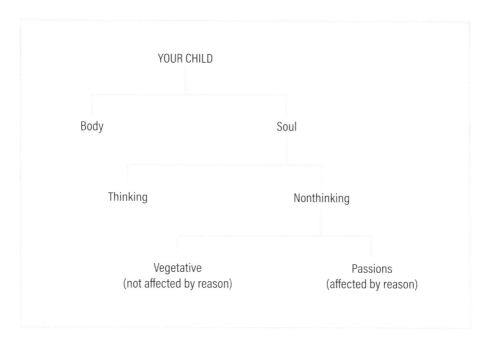

The people in your family, believe it or not, are rational creatures. You must learn to think about *their* thinking.

What are they thinking of when conflict arises? What thoughts push them to act foolishly? What thoughts occupy their minds when they get angry?

The second part of Aristotle's framework in the human soul is a little less straightforward: the non-thinking part. He divides non-thinking into two parts: vegetative and passions. The vegetative part is purely functional, dealing with nutrition, growth, and reproduction.

When it comes to relationships, the passionate part of the soul is much more interesting. Aristotle saw passions as the emotional or affective aspects of the soul. This part is responsible for feelings, desires, and emotional responses to the world around us. It encompasses a wide range of human emotions and experiences, including love, anger, fear, joy, desire, and sadness.

Aristotle tells us that passions play a significant role in human behavior and decision-making. Emotions can motivate us to act in certain ways, and they often guide our moral judgments and choices. For example, feelings of compassion can lead to acts of kindness, while anger can drive us to seek justice.

Aristotle didn't see emotions as inherently good or bad; instead, he emphasized the importance of achieving a balanced emotional life.

Aristotle was right then, and he's right now. Understanding the importance of a balanced emotional life is key in a Well-Ordered Family. Well-ordered does not mean always doing well. Expecting family members to express only positive emotions and maintain relationships operating at 100 percent satisfaction levels is unrealistic and a recipe for disaster.

It is very important in a Well-Ordered Family to realize that the goal in Aristotle's ethical framework is to cultivate virtuous emotions, or "passions," that align with moral excellence. For example, cultivating courage in the face of danger or having appropriate levels of desire for life's necessities are virtuous emotional states.

Understanding human nature is a great start to understanding the human beings, big and small, in your family. There will be very little clarity and honoring without this understanding.

YOUR GOD-GIVEN TEMPERAMENT

I love assessment tests. Who isn't fascinated by delving into personality traits? Does the test match up with your observations? Were there surprises? What does this say about you or the other?

It took a while, but business executives have finally learned that understanding an employee's natural strengths and weaknesses, likes and dislikes, goes a long way to having a happy and productive workforce.

In the old days, there was simply a job to be done, and if someone wanted a paycheck, he had better do that job. His personal affinity for the task at hand was irrelevant. A supervisor's job used to center around shoring up the worker's shortcomings. They were assumed to be many. Thankfully, we look at things differently now. Rather than addressing someone's deficiency, why not build on his strengths?

And to know exactly what those strengths are, many series of assessment tests have been born. We'll get to my favorite, but here are a few you might've heard about.

- **16PF Questionnaire:**[36] Assesses sixteen primary personality factors, providing a comprehensive view of an individual's personality. This is essential in the Myers-Briggs Test.
- **High 5 Test:**[37] Discovers what you are great at and helps you leverage your uniqueness to get greater results personally and professionally.
- **StrengthsFinder (CliftonStrengths):**[38] Identifies an individual's top strengths among thirty-four possible themes, focusing on personal strengths and talents.
- **360-Degree Feedback Assessments:**[39] Collects feedback from various sources (e.g., superiors, peers, subordinates) to evaluate an individual's performance and leadership skills.
- **Working Genius:**[40] Categorizes individuals into six distinct working types based on their work-related skills and inclinations.
- **Kolbe ATM Index:**[41] Measures an individual's instinctive method of operation, focusing on his natural strengths and tendencies for problem-solving and decision-making.

Taking assessment tests as a family can be both enjoyable and profoundly beneficial. These tests, which are often engaging and fun, provide a unique opportunity for family members to explore their individuality and learn about each other. The shared experience of taking these assessments fosters a sense of togetherness, making it a fun bonding activity.

By revealing each family member's personality traits, strengths, and preferences, these tests promote understanding and empathy. They transform family discussions into engaging conversations about what makes each member tick.

---

36 https://www.16personalities.com.

37 https://high5test.com.

38 https://www.gallup.com/cliftonstrengths/en/strengthsfinder.aspx.

39 https://www.trakstar.com/360-degree/reviews.

40 https://www.workinggenius.com.

41 https://www.kolbe.com.

The joy of discovery can reduce conflicts, with differences becoming sources of fascination rather than contention.

These assessments enhance family dynamics and help parents tailor their parenting styles to better suit their children's needs. As family members appreciate each other's unique qualities, they find common ground for bonding activities and shared goals, creating a stronger, happier family unit.

But there is one assessment that I personally have found to be foundational. I feel this assessment lies beneath all the other assessments. And it is not surprising to me that it's also the oldest assessment. It is your "temperament" according to the framework proposed by the renowned Greek physician Hippocrates around 400 BC.

TEMPERAMENT CHECK

In the intricate tapestry of family life, the threads of individual personalities are woven together to create a unique and dynamic pattern. Each family member brings his or her own distinct set of traits, strengths, and quirks to this complicated design. Yet, understanding and harmonizing these differences can often feel like an elusive challenge.

Enter the ancient wisdom of Greek temperaments, a timeless framework that has crossed over the millennia to offer invaluable insights into human nature today. The four Greek temperaments—Sanguine, Phlegmatic, Melancholic, and Choleric—can illuminate the intricate dynamics of family life.

These temperaments, rooted in the medical theories of Hippocrates, give us a lens to see the diverse array of personalities within our families. They're a way to decipher the complexities of human behavior, guide us to deeper empathy, smoother communication, and greater harmony within our most cherished social unit, the family.

We also provide tools that will empower you to navigate the beautiful mosaic of family dynamics with a newfound awareness, helping you to embrace and celebrate the rich diversity of personalities that make up your family. Whether you come to see this journey as unlocking the secret path to a previously undiscovered deep connection or as a way to incrementally increase your understanding of an already enduring bond, it will serve to strengthen the loving relationships of a Well-Ordered Family.

EXPLORING GREEK TEMPERAMENTS

The origins of the Greek temperaments date back to the fifth century BC when Hippocrates proposed a theory linking human behavior and health to bodily fluids, known as humors. According to this theory, the balance or imbalance of four primary humors—blood, phlegm, black bile, and yellow bile—determined an individual's temperament and health.

- **Sanguine:** The Sanguine temperament was associated with an excess of blood. It was believed to result in a cheerful, outgoing, and optimistic disposition. Sanguine individuals were seen as sociable and enthusiastic, often the life of the party.
- **Phlegmatic:** A surplus of phlegm was thought to produce the Phlegmatic temperament, characterized by calmness, patience, and a tendency to avoid conflict. Phlegmatic individuals were often seen as easy-going and reliable.
- **Melancholic:** An excess of black bile was linked to the Melancholic temperament. This temperament was associated with introspection, sensitivity, and a predisposition to melancholy or sadness. Melancholic individuals were often deep thinkers and artists.
- **Choleric:** An overabundance of yellow bile was believed to result in the Choleric temperament, marked by assertiveness, ambition, and a quick temper. Choleric individuals were seen as natural leaders and decision-makers.

While the ancient theory of humors has been debunked in modern medicine, the behavior essence that these temperaments symbolize has endured. Today, we view them not as biological imbalances but as archetypes that capture certain patterns of comportment, preferences, and tendencies.

Each temperament reflects a unique approach to life and interpersonal relationships. Recognizing these temperamental traits in ourselves and our family members can shed light on why we act and react the way we do. It provides a framework for understanding the inherent diversity within our families.

TEMPERAMENT STRENGTHS AND WEAKNESSES

Here is a simple list of strengths and weaknesses for each temperament. As you look through, you may feel like you have spotted yourself, your spouse, or your child.

Sanguine

Strengths:

1. Sociable and outgoing, building connections easily
2. Optimistic and enthusiastic, inspiring positivity
3. Natural entertainers, adding fun to social situations
4. Adaptability and flexibility, easing transitions
5. Creative thinkers, offering innovative ideas
6. Quick to forgive and move past conflicts
7. Energetic and enthusiastic approach to life
8. Approachable, making friends readily

Weaknesses:

1. Lack of focus and consistency
2. Impulsivity, leading to hasty decisions
3. Attention-seeking behavior, sometimes seeking the limelight
4. Difficulty with long-term commitments or routines
5. May avoid addressing serious issues to maintain positivity
6. Superficiality, sometimes lacking depth in relationships
7. Disorganization and forgetfulness
8. Struggles with self-discipline

Phlegmatic

Strengths:

1. Calm and composed, mediating conflicts effectively
2. Reliable and dependable, providing stability
3. Excellent listeners, offering emotional support
4. Diplomatic approach to problem-solving
5. Patient and tolerant, contributing to harmonious relationships
6. Open to compromise and consensus
7. Loyalty and commitment to values and traditions
8. Steady and consistent in fulfilling responsibilities

Weaknesses:
1. Tendency to avoid addressing issues directly
2. Resistance to change and reluctance to adapt
3. Passivity and indecisiveness
4. Difficulty asserting their needs or opinions
5. Risk of being overlooked or undervalued
6. Reluctance to confront conflicts
7. Complacency and resistance to personal development
8. Difficulty expressing emotions

Melancholic

Strengths:
1. Deep emotional bonds with others
2. Thoughtful decision-making and attention to detail
3. Creativity and artistic contributions
4. Loyalty and dedication to values and traditions
5. Empathetic and compassionate nature
6. Organized and detail-oriented
7. Commitment to personal growth and improvement
8. Strong work ethic and perseverance

Weaknesses:
1. Tendency toward pessimism
2. Perfectionism and frustration with imperfection
3. Overthinking problems and past events
4. Resistance to change
5. Holding grudges or dwelling on past conflicts
6. Introversion and emotional withdrawal
7. Difficulty in expressing emotions
8. Sensitivity to criticism

Choleric

Strengths:
1. Natural leadership and initiative
2. Strong problem-solving abilities

3. Ambitious and driven to achieve goals
4. Willingness to confront and address issues
5. Efficiency and effectiveness in planning and organization
6. Competitiveness in spirit that motivates others
7. Confidence and assertiveness
8. Ability to prioritize and delegate tasks

Weaknesses:
1. Quick temper and impatience
2. Control issues and reluctance to delegate
3. Excessive competitiveness
4. Risk of becoming domineering
5. Insensitivity to others' feelings
6. Goal-focused, potentially neglecting emotional needs
7. Difficulty admitting when wrong
8. Impulsivity in decision-making

HOW TO ENGAGE WITH EACH TEMPERAMENT

Understanding how to communicate and interact with different tempera-ments within a family can significantly improve relationships and create a more harmonious environment. Comprehending temperaments clues us in on how best to approach or avoid interactions in family life:

Sanguine
How to Talk and Act Toward a Sanguine:
- **Engage Actively:** Initiate conversations with enthusiasm and genuine interest. Show excitement when they share their thoughts or ideas.
- **Be Encouraging:** Provide positive feedback and praise their efforts. Acknowledge their contributions to family activities.
- **Share Experiences:** Participate in their social activities and events. Attend gatherings and outings with them to strengthen your bond.
- **Be Patient and Flexible:** Understand their spontaneous nature and be open to sudden changes in plans. Adaptability is key.
- **Celebrate Achievements:** Celebrate their achievements, no matter how small, to boost their self-esteem and motivation.

How Not to Talk and Act Toward a Sanguine:
- **Don't Be Critical:** Avoid being overly critical or negative as it can deflate their enthusiasm.
- **Don't Dominate Conversations:** Allow them to share their thoughts without constantly interjecting or dominating the conversation.
- **Avoid Strict Schedules:** Don't impose rigid schedules or routines that limit their spontaneity.
- **Respect Personal Space:** While they're social, they also need moments of solitude. Respect their need for personal space.
- **Don't Ignore Their Ideas:** Dismissing their ideas or being dismissive can be discouraging and hurtful.

Phlegmatic
How to Talk and Act Toward a Phlegmatic:
- **Be Patient and Gentle:** Approach conversations with a calm and gentle demeanor. Allow them time to express themselves.
- **Listen Actively:** Be an attentive listener, providing validation and support when they share their thoughts or concerns.
- **Acknowledge Reliability:** Express appreciation for their reliability and dependability within the family.
- **Respect Their Need for Space:** Understand their need for alone time and avoid pushing them to socialize excessively.
- **Value Their Opinions:** Include them in family discussions, showing that their opinions are valued.

How Not to Talk and Act Toward a Phlegmatic:
- **Don't Rush Them:** Avoid pressuring them to make quick decisions or changes.
- **Avoid Overstimulation:** Don't overwhelm them with too many social or high-energy activities.
- **Don't Take Advantage:** Respect their reliability and avoid taking it for granted.
- **Avoid Conflict:** Phlegmatics dislike confrontation, so avoid creating unnecessary conflicts.
- **Don't Dismiss Their Input:** Dismissing their opinions or contributions can lead to feelings of being undervalued.

Melancholic

How to Talk and Act Toward a Melancholic:

- **Be Empathetic:** Show empathy and understanding when they express deep emotions or concerns.
- **Encourage Creativity:** Support their creative endeavors and provide constructive feedback.
- **Respect Their Need for Order:** Understand their need for order and organization within the family.
- **Acknowledge Loyalty:** Recognize their loyalty and commitment to family values and traditions.
- **Offer Encouragement:** Encourage them to share their thoughts and feelings openly without fear of judgment.

How Not to Talk and Act Toward a Melancholic:

- **Don't Dismiss Their Emotions:** Avoid dismissing their emotional expressions as unnecessary or excessive.
- **Don't Criticize Creativity:** Avoid overly critical or discouraging remarks about their creative pursuits.
- **Respect Their Personal Space:** Don't disrupt their organized spaces without permission.
- **Avoid Abandoning Traditions:** Be cautious about drastically changing family traditions or routines without discussion.
- **Don't Be Insensitive:** Avoid insensitive or blunt remarks, as they may take them deeply to heart.

Choleric

How to Talk and Act Toward a Choleric:

- **Be Direct:** Communicate with clarity and directness. Present facts and arguments logically.
- **Acknowledge Leadership:** Recognize their leadership qualities and let them take charge in appropriate situations.
- **Provide Challenges:** Offer challenging tasks or responsibilities that align with their ambitions and abilities.
- **Respect Their Independence:** Give them space and autonomy to make decisions when appropriate.
- **Show Appreciation:** Express appreciation for their determination and drive in achieving family goals.

How Not to Talk and Act Toward a Choleric:
- **Avoid Micromanaging:** Don't micromanage or undermine their leadership by being overly controlling.
- **Don't Be Indecisive:** Avoid indecisiveness or excessive delays in decision-making.
- **Respect Their Competitiveness:** Don't take their competitiveness as personal attacks; they thrive on challenges.
- **Don't Undermine Their Authority:** Respect their authority and avoid undermining their leadership roles.
- **Avoid Arguments:** While direct, they can be argumentative; avoid escalating conflicts unnecessarily.

Remember that these are general guidelines, and individual variations within each temperament exist. Effective communication within a family involves flexibility, empathy, and an understanding of each family member's unique qualities and preferences.

PRIMARY AND SECONDARY TEMPERAMENTS

Understanding the concept of primary and secondary temperaments is crucial in appreciating the complexity of human personality. While some individuals significantly exhibit one dominant temperament, others may have a primary temperament with significant traits from a secondary temperament.

Secondary Temperament

A secondary temperament refers to a set of personality traits that are not as dominant as the primary temperament but still significantly influence a person's behavior and responses. These traits may emerge in specific contexts, under certain conditions, or during particular life stages.

Continuing with the previous example, someone with a primary Sanguine temperament may have secondary traits from the Choleric temperament. While he is primarily cheerful and outgoing, he might also exhibit traits such as assertiveness and ambition in specific situations.[42] As a Melancholic-Choleric myself, I can sense the secondary Choleric temperament rear up and push my Melancholy to an extreme.

The Complex Interplay

Understanding primary and secondary temperaments underscores the complexity of human personality. Few of us fit neatly into a single temperament category; instead, most people have a blend of temperamental traits to varying degrees. This blend can be influenced by genetic factors, life experiences, upbringing, and personal development.

The interplay between primary and secondary temperaments creates unique and nuanced personalities. It explains why people can behave differently in different situations or around different groups of people. For instance, a predominantly Choleric individual may display a more Sanguine demeanor when having a good time with the family, highlighting the influence of secondary temperament traits.

Embracing Individual Complexity

Understanding the presence of primary and secondary temperaments offers a more holistic view of individual personalities. It highlights the richness of human nature, acknowledging that people are not confined to rigid categories. Embracing this complexity encourages empathy and flexibility with others, as we recognize that people may respond differently based on their unique temperamental blend and the context they find themselves in. It drives home the importance of appreciating the diversity of human personalities and fostering harmonious relationships built on mutual understanding.

---

42 Some experts in this field argue that one cannot be both Sanguine and Melancholic or Choleric and Phlegmatic. While it is true these temperaments are opposites in a manner of speaking, my personal experience is that some people seem capable of being both or, more properly speaking, have one as a primary and the other as a secondary.

TEMPERAMENT RELATIONSHIPS

The interplay between temperaments is a fascinating aspect of human relationships, influencing how individuals interact, understand, and sometimes clash with one another. When examining temperamental dynamics within families, such as between spouses, siblings, or parent-child relationships, we gain insights into the complex fabric of these connections.

Spouses

In marital relationships, the interplay of temperaments can be both a source of harmony and occasional friction. Partners often bring different temperamental qualities to the relationship, creating a complementary dynamic.

For instance, a Sanguine spouse, characterized by sociability and enthusiasm, may find balance with a Phlegmatic spouse, known for calmness and dependability. The Sanguine's extroverted nature can draw the Phlegmatic out of their shell, while the Phlegmatic's patience and stability can soothe the Sanguine's occasional impulsiveness.

However, conflicts can arise when temperaments clash. For example, a Choleric partner, driven by ambition and assertiveness, may sometimes over-power a Melancholic spouse, who values introspection and emotional depth. It's crucial for couples to recognize and respect each other's temperamental differences, using them as opportunities for growth and mutual support rather than sources of tension.

Siblings

Sibling relationships are probably the best showcase for diversity of temperaments within a family. While siblings may share some temperamental traits due to common upbringing, they frequently exhibit unique combinations and strengths.

In a family with multiple siblings, you might find a mix of temperaments. For instance, one sibling may have a primary Sanguine temperament, characterized by sociability and enthusiasm, while another sibling leans toward a Phlegmatic temperament, marked by patience and reliability. The dynamic between these siblings can involve a balance of energy and stability.

When it comes to conflict, the Melancholic's sensitivity to criticism can clash with a Choleric's assertiveness and the Sanguine's penchant for poking fun. Ashley and I saw this play out in our own backyard baseball games. Our Melancholic child would be out by a mile at first base, and everyone knew it. But he couldn't admit it and would always demand a redo. Meanwhile, our Sanguine could poke the finger in jest a little too quickly. The Phlegmatic would just stay out of the fray. And so, sibling rivalries can emerge when differences in temperaments are not understood. As our children have matured, however, we have witnessed these trait differences become a source of harmonious friendship.

Parent-Child

Parent-child relationships are deeply influenced by temperamental interplay, creating a combination of shared and unique qualities within the family.

For example, a parent with a Melancholic temperament, who values introspection and creativity, may find it challenging to relate to a Sanguine child, who craves social interaction and excitement. Yet, recognizing these differences allows parents to provide a nurturing environment that supports the child's individuality.

The interplay between temperaments within parent-child relationships can influence parenting styles as well. A Phlegmatic parent, for instance, might be more patient and tolerant, while a Choleric parent may have higher expectations for achievement. Understanding these dynamics can help parents tailor their approach to meet their children's needs effectively.

In all these relationships, the key to healthy interplay between temperaments lies in recognition, empathy, and effective communication. Acknowledging that differences exist and valuing them as opportunities for growth can lead to stronger and more harmonious family dynamics. Ultimately, temperament diversity within families is a beautiful tapestry that, when embraced, enriches the shared experiences of love, growth, and connection.

"It is easy to love the people far away. It is not always easy to love those close to us."

—ST. TERESA OF CALCUTTA

CHAPTER

15

TOOLS TO IMPROVE
YOUR RELATIONSHIPS

Understanding more about God-given temperaments and human nature improves our ability to avoid and work through conflicts. But as long as families are made up of real people, there will always be conflict. It's easy to get caught in the trap of trying to avoid conflict at all costs. Conflict is not fun. It's uncomfortable. But it's not always a "bad" thing. Conflict has produced tremendous growth in both my business and family life. Two tools will help you embrace conflicts as opportunities: The Conflict Analyzer™ and The Relationship Maximizer™.

THE CONFLICT ANALYZER™

When conflict arises, particularly in the family, it's usually a result of poorly formed rationality and out-of-control passions. Have you ever had conflict with a loved one, left the room, and said to yourself, "What in the world just happened?" Join the club.

When you have conflict with a spouse, a child, or anyone, you have at least four realities converging: your own thoughts and feelings and the other person's thoughts and feelings, not to mention each person's natural temperaments. Conflict seems so confusing because we don't always understand our own thoughts and feelings, and we don't even attempt to understand the other person's thoughts and feelings. Dissecting these underlying causes for conflict and bringing them to conscious attention can help you figure out why the conflict happened and how to avoid it in the future.

The Conflict Analyzer™ delves into the thoughts and feelings that created the conflict. Analyzing the situation will help you realize how you can be at your very best the next time something similar occurs. The Conflict Analyzer™ is a valuable tool in various situations where understanding and improving communication is essential.

- **Family Conflicts:** Use this tool after heated family discussions to uncover underlying issues, empathize with each other, and find common ground for resolution.
- **Workplace Disagreements:** Employ this tool to dissect workplace disputes, fostering a more harmonious and productive work environment.
- **Relationship Challenges:** Couples can utilize this tool to decode arguments, enhance empathy, and strengthen their connection.
- **Parent-Child Interactions:** Parents can analyze conversations with their children to adapt their parenting styles and maintain healthy family dynamics.

The next time you have a conflict (and no one goes through life without them), give yourself a few minutes to break down what happened. Complete each section honestly and consider sharing findings for open dialogue and conflict resolution. It's a tool for personal growth, fostering healthier relationships, and preventing recurrent misunderstandings.

THE CONFLICT ANALYZER™

1. The Conversation

2. What I actually said or did

5. What the other actually said or did

3. What I was thinking

6. What the other was likely thinking

4. What I was feeling

7. What the other was likely feeling

8. What worked well

9. What did not work well

11. How I would've handled this on my best day

10. Do any amends need to be made?

12. How this situation is likely to repeat

13. How I will handle the situation next time

THE CONFLICT ANALYZER™ INSTRUCTIONS

1. The Conversation

Begin by filling in a brief description of the conflict. Include details like the topic, who was involved, and any immediate results or outcomes on your mind.

2. What I Actually Said or Did

Reflect on your actions and words during the conflict. Describe them honestly and objectively.

3. What I Was Thinking

Explore your thoughts during the conflict. What were your internal narratives, assumptions, or judgments?

4. What I Was Feeling

Identify your emotions throughout the conflict. Be honest about your feelings, whether they were frustration, anger, sadness, or something else.

5. What the Other Person Actually Said or Did

Document the actions and words of the other person involved in the conflict.

6. What the Other Was Likely Thinking

Consider what might have been going on in the other person's mind during the conflict. Try to empathize with his or her perspective.

7. What the Other Was Likely Feeling

Speculate about the emotions the other person was feeling during the conflict.

8. What Worked Well

Highlight any aspects of the interaction that went smoothly or were effective in achieving your goals or maintaining a positive atmosphere.

9. What Didn't Work Well

Acknowledge areas where the conversation could have been improved, where miscommunications occurred, or where emotions escalated.

10. Do Any Amends Need To Be Made?

Based on your analysis, identify actionable steps to enhance future conversations or to address any lingering issues from this one.

11. How I Would Have Handled This on My Best Day

Imagine your ideal response or behavior during the conflict. Consider how you would have handled it at your best.

12. How This Situation Is Likely to Repeat Itself

Anticipate whether similar conflicts may arise in the future with this person or in similar contexts.

13. How I Will Handle This Next Time

Summarize your plan for approaching this situation differently in the future. Include strategies for better communication and conflict resolution.

By systematically working through these steps, The Conflict Analyzer™ can help you gain deeper insights into your interactions and pave the way for more effective, empathetic, and productive conversations.

THE RELATIONSHIP MAXIMIZER™

Relationships are a tricky thing. Ultimately, however, they are an arrangement between people seeking a common goal. If you have a partnership in business, you have the stated goal of accomplishing the mission of your business. If you are on a football team, the relationship between the center and the quarterback has a very particular purpose. On one level, it is the same as the relationship between the wide receiver and the quarterback, but on another level, it is distinctive.

It is a tragic reality that we often analyze our business and social relationships more than our own family relationships. This is partly because business relationships are obviously transactive. When profit or fun is involved, we naturally articulate the relationship's purpose and spend energy on improving it. The purpose of family relationships is deeper and can seem murkier. We often do not analyze our relationships with our spouse in marriage or with our children until we are sitting in front of a counselor because all hell has broken loose.

Why not bring clarity to the relationship now?

In The Relationship Maximizer™, choose an important relationship, such as with your spouse, your child, or perhaps a parent. You can even choose God! I'd say *that* relationship is pretty important, wouldn't you?

THE RELATIONSHIP MAXIMIZER™

1. Purpose

2. Current State

HOW I SHOW _____ WHAT HE/SHE MEANS TO ME

HOW I FAIL TO SHOW IT

HOW _____ SHOWS ME WHAT I MEAN TO HIM/HER

HOW I FAIL TO SEE IT

THE RELATIONSHIP MAXIMIZER™

3. Future State

DESIRED OUTCOMES

-
-
-

ACTION ITEMS

-
-
-

Perhaps you want to take this particular relationship to the next level. In the next five minutes, this tool can help you do so.

Purpose

Defining the purpose of the relationship sounds easy, but it's often hard to nail it down. It can be elusive. What is the *real* purpose of your marriage? What is the real purpose of your relationship with God, or with your five-year-old, or your twenty-five-year-old? Perhaps you have difficult extended family conflict, such as with a half-brother, a parent, or an estranged sister-in-law. Whatever it may be, it *has* a purpose. And you will not truly find clarity in those happy or sad relationships until you get specific about their purpose.

Maybe you'll find yourself defining the purpose of your relationship with your son a little differently than with your daughter. Or perhaps you have one very aggressive son and one very laid-back son. These purposes might be different as well.

A friendly suggestion on stating purposes: If you are a faith-based person, as I am, it is tempting to answer everything with "To get to heaven." While this may be true, it is not particularly helpful in dealing with the specifics. Yes, the primary purpose of my relationship with my wife is to assist in her eternal salvation. That's what I signed up for! And the same is true for my kids. But the relationships are so different that I am served well to make the purpose more particular. Try to provide some specific and action-oriented words in your purpose statement for marriage.

- "To build a loving and supportive marriage, dedicated to holiness, with shared values, in order to foster a loving, happy, and harmonious home."
- "To create a stable and nurturing environment where each other's spiritual well-being is given primacy overall, and each other's personal goals are supported in a charitable manner."
- "To forge the most powerful bond two humans can have, with a commitment that transcends any sickness or suffering, any trial or tribulation, so that personal happiness can be found in the total giving of oneself to another."

These are examples. Take time to craft your own. Be intentional about your purpose in each relationship you are analyzing.

Current State

Under Current State, begin with articulating what this person means to you. Be generous. Why? Because writing about the importance of someone you're in conflict with is like going grocery shopping when you're hungry: a little dangerous! Be aware of your present emotions. "Know thyself" particularly when thyself is grouchy. Consider what this person means to you on your best day.

Follow the arrow downward and ask yourself: "How do I show this person what he or she means to me?" Do you expect the other to read your mind? Do you find it isn't necessary to show it because the meaning is understood? (Hint: be very careful when coming to that conclusion!) Or do you need to step up the outward expression of the other's importance in your life? Also, ask: "How do I fail to show it?" Is there a particular bad behavior that communicates the opposite of what the person actually means to you? Perhaps the other person is obnoxious, but you really do love him or her. Do you ever communicate that you love the other person, or just that he or she is obnoxious? Admittedly, this stuff is not for the faint of heart. Taking a look at yourself can hard and requires humility.

Move to the right column and ask yourself what you mean to the other person. It's always humbling for me to realize that I mean more to certain people than they mean to me. There's nothing wrong with this, *per se*. It just is. And there are plenty of people who mean more to me than I mean to them. Life is not equal in all areas.

For example, I love all my children with all my heart. But the reality is that I have fifteen at the time I am writing this book. And yet, each one of them has only one father! It's easy to be angry with one kid, have my attention consumed by another, and conveniently ignore the kid I have issues with. I constantly fight this. One might say it is my particular battle as a father. And one way to gain control is to remember that my kids have only one dad. That is me.

Following the arrow downward, we should determine "How _____ shows it" and "How I fail to see it." Most likely, your loved ones show you they love you. They show you how important you are to them. But given we are a sinful race, we allow our resentments to cover up our deeper appreciations.

Help your family members by looking past their expressions of resentment, and peer deep into what you truly mean to them. In fact, as counterintuitive as this sounds, often those who love you the most are the least likely to show it. As the old saying goes, familiarity breeds contempt. Well, we are very familiar with our loved ones. We take them for granted. We imagine that they can somehow look past our eyes and into our hearts. As a result, we fail to express how much they mean to us. If this is true for you, know that it is true for others. That's why it's especially important for you to know "How you fail to see it."

The Ideal State

This section might be a little surprising.

As businesses do in a process improvement exercise, we ought to conceptualize the ideal state of a relationship. The ideal state might be out of reach. It may always be out of reach. Again, we are flawed, sinful creatures. It is important, however, to figure out what the ideal is for this particular relationship at this point in your life, even if it seems unobtainable.

I truly hope you see the ideal marriage and ideal relationship with your children in a vibrant and deep and intimate way. I hope your relationship with your closest friends takes on a beautiful and sacred meaning in your life.

It's worth noting, however, that not all relationships can live up to this standard. Some relationships with, say, extended family or old friends might need some healthy distance. As you progress through different stages of life, as your kids grow, as your personal expectations transcend previous ones, you may find yourself limited in how much you can give to people from your past. This does not mean the person is less important, but it might mean the relationship is less important to you. For me, the ideal relationship with certain people means checking up on them once a year. For some, it means talking to them four times a year. For some, it means dinner with them twice a year. That is ideal for me. Maybe they want more. But I can't always give more than that. I need to articulate this to myself first so that I can begin making headway toward that ideal state. I readily admit that relationships cannot be boiled down to a certain amount of encounters per year. But it is my deeply held tenet that measurables can provide information about qualitative matters. In this case, signs for that the relationship is reaching its ideal state.

Future State

The future state is something much closer than the ideal state. It might take time to get to the ideal state, but you can make headway immediately on the future state. This is making the small improvements that are within your control. This might be why you bought this book.

Maybe your ideal state for marriage is a relationship in which your deepest spiritual desires and experiences are shared openly with your spouse, where the shame of hypocrisy is no longer in your way, and you finally feel that you can be your truest self with the person you married many years ago. In reality, this will not be accomplished overnight. But in the future state section of this tool, you can take a step tomorrow. First, perhaps you can say something as simple as, "I hope I can start having more spiritual conversations with you. The chaos of the family seems to get in the way. Maybe we can find a way around that." Or maybe you start having The Weekly Marriage Check-In™ proposed earlier. That simple agenda will begin the process of opening up to each other. It can be a slow process sometimes punctuated by rapid advance, sometimes not. That's why visualizing the future state can be a powerful tool for steady change.

To reach this future state, there are specific outcomes you desire and specific action items to put in place immediately. Take a few minutes to consider what the outcomes of this future state would look like. Then, list a few actions you need to take immediately to begin working toward those outcomes.

\

CONCLUSION

Hopefully, you now you have a better understanding of why relationships are so important in a Well-Ordered Family and a few practical tools to help keep those bonds as close- knit as they need to be. They form the most important environments in which our family systems operate. In fact, you might even say those systems are "for" fostering relationships.

So far we've talked about Vision, Unity, Systems, Metrics, and Relationships. But there is one last part to having a Well-Ordered Family, and that is decision making and problem solving. Discernment is our final step in the Family Management System.

PART - 6

DISCERNMENT

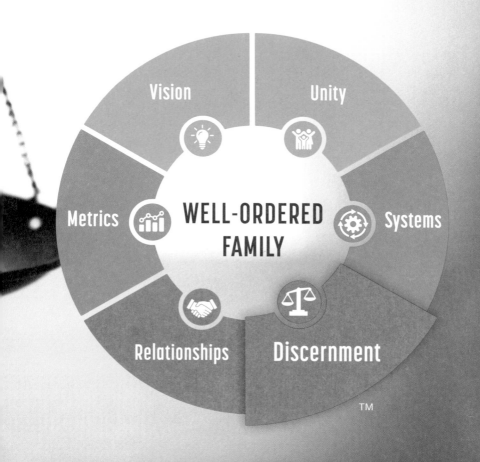

"As the family goes, so goes the nation and so goes the whole world."

–POPE ST. JOHN PAUL II

CHAPTER

16

EVERY DECISION
IS SPIRITUAL

Family holds a sacred place in our world. Here, we forge bonds that shape our identities, nurture our souls, and provide a haven of love and support. It is also within these familial ties where we make decisions that touch the core of our being. It's the essence of decision making, laden with profound implications and intricate complexities. This has led me to embrace the specialized term "discernment" in the exploration of family dynamics.

WHY DISCERNMENT IS SPIRITUAL

The term "discernment" carries a spiritual resonance for Christians in particular, invoking a deeper contemplation of the choices we make and the paths we tread. Rooted in the Latin word *discernere*, meaning "to separate" or "to distinguish," discernment invites us to traverse the labyrinth of options, shedding light on the avenues that align with our values, beliefs, and higher calling. For us Christians, in this process of discernment we connect with the

Lord, seeking His will before our own. In other words, we don't think things happen randomly. We consider God's will discoverable—and we want to do God's will. To go against it is sinful.

If you'd rather avoid these terms, you can conceive of a moral natural law in this fashion. One should not spend one's life trying to swim *up* a waterfall!

In the context of family life, the significance of discernment is magnified. Every decision we encounter within the realm of our family unit holds profound spiritual implications. From the choice of a weekend activity to the selection of a school for our children, the decisions we make help write our family's narrative. These choices not only reflect our values but also shape the environment in which our loved ones flourish.

Decisions we make don't just determine what we do; they can become who we are. We must look beyond our individual perspectives and embrace a holistic approach to decision making—one that considers the well-being of every member of our family. Discernment calls us to navigate the delicate balance between personal aspirations and collective harmony. Family life has a purpose. We can know that purpose and move toward it.

THE DIFFERENCE BETWEEN DECISION MAKING AND PROBLEM SOLVING

Decision-making tools and problem-solving tools are related, but they serve slightly different purposes and focus on different aspects of addressing challenges.

Decision-Making Tools: Imagine you have multiple options to choose from, and you need to pick the best one, such as which family car to purchase. Decision-making tools help you compare these options and make a choice. They provide a structured way to evaluate the pros and cons of each option, consider factors like costs, benefits, risks, and outcomes, and then decide which option aligns best with your goals and preferences. These tools assist you in making a choice from among several alternatives.

Problem-Solving Tools: Now, picture a situation where you're facing a challenge or a puzzle and you need to find a solution, such as "Dad is very unhappy in his job." Problem-solving tools help you work through the steps needed to come up with a solution to a particular problem. They guide you

in understanding the problem, brainstorming ideas, analyzing the root causes, and developing strategies to address it. These tools are useful when you're
trying to figure out how to overcome obstacles or resolve specific issues.

In essence, while decision-making tools assist you in choosing the best
option from a set of alternatives, problem-solving tools guide you in finding
solutions to challenges or issues you're facing when the choices are not either/
or. They can often work together, as solving a problem might involve making
decisions along the way, and making a decision could be part of solving a larger problem. So, while they're not exactly the same thing, they complement
each other and are both important in navigating various situations effectively.

"In any moment of decision, the best thing you can do is the right thing, the next best thing is the wrong thing, and the worst thing you can do is nothing."

–THEODORE ROOSEVELT

DECISION-MAKING TOOLS FOR FAMILY LIFE

From the mundane choices of daily routines to the profound, life-altering moments, decisions define a family's existence. This chapter is dedicated to empowering families with the tools and strategies needed to navigate the labyrinth of choices that determine our domestic landscape.

Families are complex ecosystems where individual desires, needs, and aspirations intersect. They are crucibles of love, understanding, and sometimes, conflict. Within this intricate web, decisions act as catalysts that can either fortify the bonds or strain the ties. Choices about education, finances, leisure, and more profoundly, values and priorities, all shape the family's course.

Just like other organizations, families can benefit from structured approaches to decision making. I hope by this point I've managed to convince you! In the following pages, we present multiple tools, each offering a unique perspective and method, to provide you with a comprehensive arsenal in the decision-making process. Whether it's choosing the right school for your children, managing family finances, or resolving conflicts with empathy, these tools will be your trusted companions.

THE FAMILY FOCUS BOX™

In the vast landscape of family life, prioritizing tasks can often feel like traversing a maze with no clear path. Enter The Family Focus Box™, your compass for effective decision making in the bustling world of family dynamics.

At its core, The Family Focus Box™ is a modified version of that old management standby, the Eisenhower Matrix, a time-tested tool for sorting tasks into four quadrants based on their urgency and

---

THE FAMILY FOCUS BOX™

	URGENT	NOT URGENT
IMPORTANT	**Do Now** *Go to doctor* *Fix dryer*	**Do Next** *Plan vacation* *Set up college fund*
NOT IMPORTANT	**Do Last** *Clean out garage* *Check social media*	**Do Never** *Rewatch game* *Argue on social media*

---

importance. In our adaptation, we'll show you how this can help your family identify what truly matters.

Do Now: These are the tasks demanding immediate attention and are of utmost importance. In family life, this might include addressing urgent medical needs, handling a broken appliance, or resolving an imminent conflict. The Family Focus Box™ ensures these vital issues don't slip through the cracks, allowing your family to act swiftly and decisively.

Do Next: Here, we find tasks that are important but not necessarily urgent. This quadrant holds the activities that contribute to your family's long-term goals and well-being, like planning for vacations, setting up a college fund, or nurturing relationships. By recognizing the significance of these

THE FAMILY FOCUS BOX™

	URGENT	NOT URGENT
IMPORTANT	Do Now	Do Next
NOT IMPORTANT	Do Last	Do Never

tasks, you prevent them from being overshadowed by the constant barrage of urgent matters.

Do Last: These are tasks that lack urgency and importance. They often masquerade as distractions and can steal precious time if they are not identified.

Think of scrolling through social media for hours or obsessively reorganizing the garage or bedrooms. The Family Focus Box™ sends these time-wasters to the back burner, allowing your family to focus on what counts.

Do Never: This quadrant has tasks that are neither urgent nor important. They can be likened to mental clutter, taking up valuable mental space that could be better used elsewhere. By recognizing and eliminating these tasks, your family can free up time and energy for endeavors that enrich your lives. Don't dismiss this step. It is a sign of your family's uniqueness. What is a total waste of time for one family might have value to another, and vice versa.

The power of The Family Focus Box™ lies not just in its conceptual simplicity but in its practical application within the family as a whole. Consider incorporating the matrix into family meetings. Perhaps you feel overwhelmed with too many items on the chore list. Gather the family together and list the items on the matrix as a visual aid. Literally seeing the task on the matrix is often eye-opening. And allowing other family members to express their opinions on where items should go can be beneficial.

Once tasks are placed on the matrix, you can delegate who is accountable for what. The one designated as the task's champion will now have a better sense of the importance and urgency of the task assigned to him. Everyone likes clarity. It provides meaning behind what can otherwise seem to be blind obedience to dictum.

For this reason, The Family Focus Box™ is an excellent tool for teaching children about decision making. It helps them understand the concepts of urgency and importance, instilling valuable life skills from an early age. Even the smallest of children can understand the difference in urgency and importance. And they absolutely love seeing the tasks on a visual tool in front of them.

By implementing The Family Focus Box™, you equip your family with a potent tool for decisionmaking, time management, and goal setting. It transforms the chaos of daily life into a well-ordered symphony where each task finds its harmonious place, allowing your family to flourish. In the subsequent sections of this chapter, we'll explore additional decision-making tools and strategies, enhancing your family's ability to navigate the complexities of life with confidence and purpose.

PROS AND CONS

At first glance, the pros and cons list might seem like the most obvious tool in the decision-making toolbox. After all, who needs a guide to tell them that listing the good stuff and the not-so-good stuff about a choice is a good idea, right? It's like saying, "Hey, before you make a decision, how about you think about the decision?" Thank you, Professor Obvious.

But here's the thing. Sometimes, the most straightforward tools are the most powerful ones. Even though it's as basic as making a peanut butter and jelly sandwich, the pros and cons list is like the Swiss Army knife of decision making. It might be simple, but it is more valuable for families than people might realize.

Picture this: You and your family are facing a decision. It could be seemingly small, like choosing a vacation spot, or something that'll shake things up, like moving to a new city. You all have your thoughts swirling around, but they're like those pesky fireflies on a summer night—hard to catch and even harder to understand.

Now, grab that trusty pros and cons list. Start jotting down the good stuff—the pros—and the not-so-good stuff—the cons. Suddenly, those buzzing thoughts start making sense. You see them on paper, and it's like turning on a light in a dark room.

It's not just about seeing the words; it's about understanding what really matters to your family. You might realize that the vacation spot with the cool theme park isn't as important as being close to nature, or that moving to a new city means more opportunities for the kids but also leaving behind your church community.

Plus, there's the magic of getting everyone on the same page. We all have different ways of thinking, but when you put it down on paper, there's little room for misinterpreting. You're all looking at the same list, and that can spark great family discussions.

THE FAMILY PROS AND CONS LIST	
Main Issue: Moving to a New City	
PROS	**CONS**
-Fresh start -More convenience, closer to stores, school, etc. -Will foster kids' social skills, expand family's social network -More opportunities for kids, academics & extracurricular activities	-Will be farther away from extended family -Must change churches, lose current church community -Kids lose close contact with friends they've grown up with - Must find suitable new house/ neighborhood and move -Security of neighborhood and neighbor relationships gone/must be reestablished -Dad no longer 10 minutes from the office -Won't get to enjoy recent home/ outdoor improvements -Likely to have less indoor/outdoor space

And let's not forget that a systemic list forces you to articulate your thoughts. You can't just say, "I don't know; it just feels right." Nope, you've got to explain why it feels right, and that can be eye-opening. Sometimes what feels right might not make much sense when you put it in words.

The Family Pros and Cons List might be about as basic as it gets, but sometimes the simplest tools are the ones that get the job done best. It's like that trusty hammer in your toolbox; it's not flashy, but when you need to hang a picture or build a treehouse, it's your go-to tool. The Family Pros and Cons List? It's your trusty decision-making tool helping your family build a path forward one choice at a time.

The Family Pros and Cons List is most effective when an issue works out to be heavily weighted on one side. In our example of moving to a new

THE FAMILY PROS AND CONS LIST	
Main Issue:	
PROS	**CONS**

city, there are twice as many cons as there are pros. The list makes it pretty obvious that moving isn't the right decision. But what about when an issue isn't so obvious?

THE FAMILY CBA™

Before taking on a new project, businesses map out a Cost-Benefit Analysis (CBA) to make sure it makes sense. No sane manager or CEO would blindly dump hundreds or thousands of dollars into a new initiative without justifying the cost beforehand. And so, all the potential costs of a project are added up and weighed against the potential revenues that might be generated. The result of the analysis will hopefully make it clear which decision the business should make. I think families can do something very similar when faced with a tough decision.

The Family CBA™ is the tool to use when the question is whether you should do something or not. Sometimes a simple pros and cons list isn't enough to decide. Some issues have numerous pros and cons, but the value of each is not immediately obvious.

Not all pros and cons have the same value. That's where further analysis is required. Don't worry. This isn't as difficult as it sounds. And it can actually be fun. It requires your family to put a numerical value on something that might not be obvious. Nobody thinks that the NFL annual draft assigns ultimate value to each football player either as an athlete or a man, but it offers a useful ordering when a decision must be made—and it's fun!

Ashley and I recently used this tool to help us decide whether to turn our garage into a family living space. Take a gander.

First, we looked at the potential costs of turning our garage into a family living space. We came up with a handful of categories, briefly described them, and then estimated the costs. Notice there are hard costs here, like construction materials and labor. These were relatively easy to estimate. It's the soft costs that are trickier. What does the disruption of a construction

THE FAMILY CBA™					
COSTS			**BENEFITS**		
Category	Description	Value	Category	Description	Value
Construction	Raw materials & labor	20K	Second living space	Additional space to gather as a family	30K
Lose garage	Devalues home and less storage space	5K	Place to store musical instruments	Perfect for piano & guitar	5K
Family disruption	Will need to move out of the house during construction	5K	Added study space	Won't have to use kitchen table for homework	5K
Ashley's time	Will have to pick out materials, manage process	7K	Extra bedroom	Can use current bonus room as a bedroom	5K
Total		37K	Total		45K

zone "cost" my family? How much will it "cost" my family when Ashley is devoting some of her time to this project in addition to homeschooling or otherwise managing the family?

The point when estimating these costs isn't to come up with the exact correct number but rather to estimate the costs relative to the other numbers. For instance, when coming up with a number to quantify adding a second living space to our house, Ashley suggested we put an annual value on the additional space and multiply by how many years we plan on living in our house. We plan on being in our house for thirty more years, and I estimated the value of another living space at a thousand dollars a year. We wrote down 30K as the benefit value for a second living space. Is this ultimately true? Maybe. But it did help us view the decision with a long-term perspective.

Try to focus less about these precise values and focus more on getting the ideas on paper, weighing their potential value, and discussing those categories relative to the others.

The Family CBA™ helped Ashley and I conclude that converting our garage into a second living space was the right move for our family. And by using this tool, it took a lot of stress and anxiety out of the decision-making process.

THE FAMILY CBA™					
COSTS			BENEFITS		
Category	Description	Value	Category	Description	Value
Total			Total		

THE FAMILY DECISION MATRIX™

The Family Pros and Cons List and The Family CBA™ are most helpful when choosing whether to do something or not. "To do, or not to do: that is the question," to paraphrase Hamlet. But what about choosing between two *similar* options? How many times in life do we find ourselves trying to decide between option A and option B? If you are anything like me, you find yourself wallowing in indecision. As a melancholic, I am prone to paralysis-by-analysis. A tool that I've found particularly helpful is a decision matrix. Hey, if Hamlet had possessed such a tool, maybe the stage wouldn't be littered with bodies at the end of Shakespeare's play!

A decision matrix, also known as a decision-making matrix, is a systematic tool used to evaluate and prioritize a set of options or alternatives based on multiple criteria or factors. It provides a structured framework for decision making by allowing individuals or groups to objectively compare various choices and assess their strengths and weaknesses in relation to specific criteria.

Here's the secret: you run a decision matrix in your head every single day. The trick, however, is to formalize it. Much of the stress will melt away. The communication will be cut to a minimum. And family members will get on the same page.

1. **Identify Criteria:** First, establish a list of criteria or factors that are relevant to your decision. These criteria should be measurable and relevant to the problem or choice at hand. For example, if you're deciding between different job offers, criteria might include salary, location, job responsibilities, and company culture.
2. **Assign Weights:** Assign a weight or importance score to each criterion to indicate its relative significance. These weights reflect the importance of each criterion in the final decision. A scale of one to ten is commonly used, with ten being the highest importance.
3. **List Alternatives:** Identify all the alternatives or options you want to evaluate. These are the different choices or solutions you're considering.
4. **Evaluate Alternatives:** For each alternative, assess how well it performs on each criterion. Use a numerical scale, such as one to five or one to ten, to rate each alternative's performance on each criterion.

5. **Calculate Scores:** Multiply the scores for each alternative by the corresponding weight for each criterion. Then, sum these weighted scores to obtain a total score for each alternative.
6. **Select the Best Option:** The alternative with the highest total score is considered the best choice based on the established criteria.

Decision matrices are especially useful when dealing with complex decisions that involve multiple factors and trade-offs. They provide a structured way to compare and contrast alternatives, helping individuals or groups make informed decisions that align with their priorities and goals.

Scenario: You're choosing between three different cars to purchase based on criteria such as price, fuel efficiency, safety, and cargo space—a decision modern families face all the time. Here's how to approach it with a decision matrix.

- Each criterion (Price, Fuel Efficiency, Safety, and Cargo Space) is assigned a weight using a scale from one to ten based on its importance to the decision-maker.
- Each car (Car A, Car B, and Car C) is evaluated and scored on each criterion using a scale from one to ten.
- The Total Value for each car is calculated by multiplying the criterion score by the criterion weight and then summing these values.
- Car B has the highest total value (233), making it the recommended choice based on the established criteria.

"Of course it turns out to be the minivan," you sigh as you fork over the cash.

THE FAMILY DECISION MATRIX™							
Criteria	Weight (1-10)	Car A	A Value	Car B	B Value	Car C	C Value
Price	8	6	48	7	56	6	48
Fuel Efficiency	7	5	35	9	63	6	42
Safety	9	9	81	8	72	7	63
Cargo Space	6	4	24	7	42	8	48
Total Value			188		233		201

Here is a blank template your family can use:

THE FAMILY DECISION MATRIX™			
Criteria	Weight	Option A	A Value
Total Value			

THE FAMILY DECISION MATRIX™			
Option B	B Value	Option C	C Value

CONCLUSION

Decision making isn't just about picking what's for dinner or where to spend your next vacation; it's about crafting the path of your family's journey. In this chapter, we've explored several tools to help you navigate this essential task: The Family Focus Box™, the pros and cons list, and The Family Decision Matrix™.

They might seem like simple tools, but then so are pliers and screwdrivers. Their impact on your family's discernment process can be profound. Take them out of the box. Use them!

These tools are like compasses in the wilderness of choices, guiding you toward decisions that align with your family's values, dreams, and aspirations. They allow you to step back and see the bigger picture, providing clarity amid the chaos of options. Each tool offers a unique perspective, whether it's prioritizing urgency and importance, weighing the pros and cons, or quantifying choices with precision.

Moreover, these tools hold a spiritual significance within the context of discernment. They invite your family to reflect on its purpose, its core values, and its place in the world. By using them, you engage in a process of self-discovery and alignment with a higher purpose. Through these tools, you can discern not only what's right for your family but also how your choices align with your spiritual journey.

Remember that discernment is the foundation upon which effective problem solving is built. The same tools you've learned here will serve as beacons of wisdom when facing challenges within your family. Just as a skilled craftsman relies on the right tools to create a masterpiece, so too can your family create a life filled with purpose, harmony, and love.

So, take these decision-making tools with you, let them become a part of your family's toolkit for life, and as you embark on the journey of problem solving, may you find strength, unity, and the joy of living a well-ordered family life.

18

PROBLEM-SOLVING TOOLS FOR FAMILY LIFE

Navigating the intricate web of family life can be both a rewarding and challenging journey. While families share love, bonds, and cherished moments, they are not immune to conflicts, disagreements, and complex issues. These challenges are an inevitable part of family dynamics, and how a family responds to them can significantly impact its overall well-being. This chapter is dedicated to equipping you with problem-solving tools tailored to the unique context of family life.

THE FAMILY AS A PROBLEM-SOLVING UNIT

I am always surprised at how certain kids contribute to problem solving in my house. David, for example, is ten years old. He is the posterchild of the rambunctious little boy and sometimes the annoying little brother who makes it his life goal to frustrate his older sisters.

But give the kid some slack. He has two older sisters right above him and four younger sisters below. He's a boy-sandwich!

Often David's only refuge is his six-year old twin brothers. David should probably be living like his patron, King David, who was fighting off wolves and lions in the wilderness with a slingshot at ten years old. He is just not built to be stuck inside playing games with a pack of girls.

Yet one thing my wife and I have realized is that David has an unusual gift for problem solving. His creative mind envisions how to quickly jerry-rig anything. At first, I thought his suggestions and his insistence on inserting himself into situations was annoying. But when I took the time to listen to his words, I noticed that he's actively engaged in proposing solutions.

It was natural for him. After all, he was doing this all day as he fit into work and play with his many sisters.

Ashley and I began to embrace this. "David, how would you organize the tools in the barn?" "David, can you figure out a way to keep the remote control from getting lost all the time?"

David is human duct tape. His so-called annoying side is actually native intelligence looking for an outlet. Now we try to keep him problem solving. It's essential to his well-being and a benefit to ours. One day, he might solve a problem like cancer or contained nuclear fusion. Who knows?

I've also noticed that our sanguine children, those who are lively, friendly, socially smooth, and the life of the party are of extreme benefit in problem solving. To be clear, they are only indifferently gifted at the physical work portion of a job. But their emotional intelligence helps family conversations run smoothly. They can enter into the family dynamic to help people get along and work as a team.

My choleric kids often might not say a lot; they might not have a bunch of ideas on how to solve a problem, but boy can they produce. They are the workhorses and will get the job done.

One of my older kids, Patrick, can build anything, including the home office that I am enjoying right now, which he created over a series of weeks of careful labor. He purchased plans for an outdoor shed and modified them to become a home office.

It is my paradise. You definitely want Patrick around for key parts of problem solving. But communication is not his strong suit.

One day, Ashley and I were sitting in the kitchen when Patrick (twelve years old at the time) came running inside frantically:

"It's like Aiden has a third eye!!!"

We looked at each other. "What?"

"It's Aiden. It's like he has a third eye!!!"

"Er, Patrick. What the heck are you talking about?"

Just then, Peter (nine years old) ran in to tell us, "Aiden got hit in the face with a metal baseball bat."

We hurry outside to find Aiden (fourteen at the time) pushing himself up off the ground and holding his forehead. Our little genius had decided to have his brother throw a big, rubber exercise ball so he could hit it with the baseball bat. The bat immediately bounced back and hit Aiden smack in the forehead.

Patrick brilliantly sees the world through metaphors. "Aiden has a third eye" meant to him that Aiden had a huge bump growing fast on his forehead, as if he had a third eye. This talent is useful in many ways, but perhaps not for communicating precise emergency information succinctly.

Our son Peter may lack some of the talent Patrick has in the metaphor department, but in this case, Peter was chock full of common sense and useful communication skills. He told us what we needed to know and made it crystal clear. (On the other hand, Peter has not built his dear old dad a home office.)

Every family member contributes to solving problems in a different way (and often helps create the problem to begin with!).

In every family, large or small, conflicts and problems arise. Maybe you have minor disagreements about daily routines or more significant challenges like financial issues, parenting dilemmas, or strained relationships. How a family addresses these challenges can serve to strengthen or weaken the most cherished bonds we have. Families are, in essence, problem-solving units. Each member brings unique perspectives, values, and emotions into the mix, creating a diverse range of thoughts and feelings. Successfully navigating these complexities requires a combination of empathy, communication skills, and, crucially, effective problem-solving techniques.

THE SIGNIFICANCE OF EFFECTIVE PROBLEM SOLVING

Effective problem solving is not just about resolving conflicts; it's about promoting understanding, empathy, and unity within the family. When handled well, problem solving doesn't just resolve a particular issue, but provides follow-on benefits.

- **Strengthens Family Bonds:** By addressing challenges openly and respectfully, families can foster trust and stronger connections among their members.
- **Teaches Valuable Life Skills:** Problem solving within the family setting provides an ideal platform for children and adolescents to learn essential life skills, including conflict resolution, communication, and decision making.
- **Reduces Stress and Tension:** Unresolved problems and conflicts can lead to stress and tension within the family. Addressing these issues head-on can alleviate these emotional burdens.
- **Enhances Well-Being:** A family that can effectively address its challenges tends to experience greater overall well-being and satisfaction.

THE ROAD AHEAD

Let's explore two powerful problem-solving tools that families can incorporate into their lives. These tools are versatile and adaptable, making them suitable for addressing a wide range of family-related issues.

1. **The Five Whys:** This technique involves asking "why?" multiple times to uncover the root causes of a problem. It encourages deep exploration and understanding of issues.
2. **The 80/20 Principle (Pareto Principle):** This principle suggests that roughly 80 percent of effects result from 20 percent of causes. Families can use this to prioritize and focus their efforts on the most critical issues.

It's important to remember that these techniques are not just about resolving conflicts but also about creating a harmonious and thriving family environment. They empower you to approach challenges as opportunities for growth and understanding.

In the sections that follow, we will delve into each of these tools, offering practical guidance, real-life examples, and case studies to illustrate their application within family life. By the end of this chapter, you will be equipped with a toolkit to tackle family issues with confidence and grace, strengthening the bonds that hold your family together.

THE FIVE WHYS

The Jefferson Memorial Mystery: A Lesson in Problem Solving

Picture yourself standing before the majestic Jefferson Memorial in Washington, DC. The radiant white exterior highlighted by its marble columns and rounded dome gleaming in the sunlight. This iconic monument has long been a symbol of American history and architecture. Yet, beneath its grandeur, an unexpected and perplexing problem once lurked: persistent bird poop.

Rather than rushing to address the issue with conventional methods, the custodians of the memorial decided to employ a systematic problem-solving technique known as The Five Whys. This approach, rooted in the heart of lean manufacturing and the Toyota Production System, proved to be an invaluable tool in solving the mystery.

The Rule of The Five Whys

The Five Whys is deceptively simple yet incredibly effective. It involves asking why five times in succession when confronted with a problem, each time probing deeper to reveal the root cause. By repeatedly asking why, you move beyond surface-level symptoms to identify the underlying issues that need attention.

In the case of the Jefferson Memorial, The Five Whys unfolded as follows:

1. **Why are there bird droppings on the memorial?**
   Because birds are roosting on the memorial's surface.
2. **Why are the birds roosting there?**
   Because they are feasting on spiders that inhabit the memorial.
3. **Why are there so many spiders?**
   Because they are attracted to the abundant gnats near the memorial.
4. **Why are there so many gnats near the memorial?**
   Because the lights around the memorial are left on at night.

5. Why are the lights left on at night?

Because no one thought to turn them off.

By methodically applying The Five Whys, the team at the Jefferson Memorial reached the root cause of the problem: the unnecessary illumination of the memorial at night. A simple change in behavior—turning off the lights—resolved the issue.

In life, all too often we battle the birds and the spiders and the gnats when all we need to do is flip a switch. Particularly in family life, the solution is often deceptively simple. But if we don't drill down to the root of a problem, then we expend a bunch of effort for little result. In this sense, it's good to be like that little child that asks, "Why? Why? Why?" In fact, experience shows me that we can almost always get to the root cause within five whys.

Applying The Five Whys to Family Life

Let's use an example to demonstrate the practical use of The Five Whys in everyday life.

In our hypothetical family, tensions have been running high resulting in constant arguments over divvying up household chores. Instead of brushing these conflicts aside, they decide to employ The Five Whys:

1. Why are we arguing so frequently?

Because we disagree on how household chores should be divided.

2. Why do we disagree on household chores?

Because we have different expectations for each other's contributions.

3. Why do we have different expectations?

Because we never clearly communicated our expectations.

4. Why didn't we communicate our expectations?

Because we assumed the other family members knew what we wanted.

5. Why did we make such assumptions?

Because we never had a family meeting to discuss our roles and expectations.

By persistently asking why, the family ultimately identifies the root cause of their constant arguments. It isn't the chores themselves; it's a lack of open communication and shared understanding of household responsibilities. Armed with this insight, they can now take actionable steps to enhance communication and set clear expectations, which could potentially reduce the frequency of their disputes.

The Five Whys method, despite its apparent simplicity, is a potent tool for exploring family issues deeply. It promotes self-reflection, uncovers underlying causes, and empowers families to engage in more effective problem solving. Just like at the Jefferson Memorial, sometimes the simplest solutions can yield profound results.

THE FIVE WHYS

WHAT IS THE PROBLEM?

1. WHY DID THIS HAPPEN?

2. WHY DID THIS HAPPEN?

3. WHY DID THIS HAPPEN?

THE FIVE WHYS

4. WHY DID THIS HAPPEN?

5. WHY DID THIS HAPPEN?

POSSIBLE SOLUTIONS & COUNTERMEASURES

WHY?

WHY?

THE 80/20 FAMILY OPTIMIZER™

Throughout the vast universe, there is a cosmic law that transcends cultures, industries, and species. This universal law is known as the 80/20 Principle, or the Pareto Principle, and it holds a profound place in our lives, offering insights into the balance and design of our world.

The 80/20 Principle, in its simplest form, states that roughly 80 percent of effects come from 20 percent of causes. This idea was first introduced by the Italian economist Vilfredo Pareto, who noticed that 80 percent of Italy's land was owned by just 20 percent of the population. However, the principle extends far beyond land ownership; it permeates our daily lives, our surroundings, and even our families.

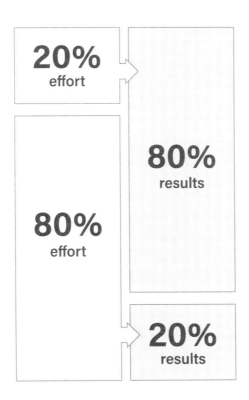

The Divine Imprint

Is the 80/20 Principle a mere coincidence, a statistical quirk? Or is there something deeper, a divine blueprint that governs the universe? Just look around.

- **Business:** Approximately 80 percent of a company's profits often come from 20 percent of its customers or products. I didn't believe this until I ran the numbers myself, but it is absolutely true. Businesses are wise to focus on those 20 percent of customers and products to maximize revenue.
- **Time Management:** People often spend 80 percent of their time on tasks that yield only 20 percent of the overall results. Identifying and prioritizing the most productive tasks can greatly increase efficiency.
- **Health and Fitness:** In many cases, 80 percent of the health benefits can be achieved through 20 percent of the exercise and dietary choices. The reverse is also true: 80 percent of your dietary problems come from only 20 percent of your food choices. Concentrate on the most effective workouts and nutritious foods.
- **Software Development:** A significant majority (around 80 percent) of software errors or bugs are typically caused by a small percentage (20 percent) of the code. Focusing on debugging these critical sections can greatly improve software quality.
- **Real Estate:** In real estate, 20 percent of the properties often account for 80 percent of the property value appreciation in a given area.
- **Social Life:** Often, 80 percent of your happiness and satisfaction come from just 20 percent of your friends, family, or social activities. Prioritize spending time with those who truly matter.

These examples show how a minority of causes tend to produce the majority of effects in multiple areas of life.

Keep in mind, the 80/20 principle doesn't rigidly require an 80/20 split. Think of it as more of a guideline that highlights a significant imbalance in cause and effect. The essence of the principle is to recognize that in many situations, the "trivial many" effects are produced by the "vital few" causes. In fact, I prefer to call this principle "The Rule of the Vital Few" to emphasize the importance of focusing efforts on the critical factors that drive the most significant impact.

Time To Optimize

The 80/20 Family Optimizer™ will help identify the twenty percent of family activities that yield 80 percent of the benefits. This tool will help you home in on what truly matters in your family.

Step 1: Identify the Best 20 Percent

Begin with introspection. Reflect on your family's daily life and list the activities that bring the most joy, growth, and harmony. These are the high-impact moments—the family dinners, heartfelt conversations, shared adventures—those rare gems that make life worthwhile.

Step 2: Strengthen the Best 20 Percent

Once you've identified these precious activities, consider how to elevate them. Allocate more time, effort, and resources to enhance these experiences.

Step 3: Identify the Worst 20 Percent

Face the harsh reality: 20 percent of the actions turn into 80 percent of the problems. List the actions, habits, or attitudes that breed discord or harm within your family. Acknowledge them with compassion, knowing that awareness is the first step toward transformation.

Step 4: Eliminate the Worst 20 Percent

Now, with newfound determination, take steps to eliminate these harmful elements. Engage your family in discussions, seek professional guidance if needed, and work collectively toward harmony.

The Divine Purpose

From the galaxies to the family hearth, the 80/20 Principle is a whisper indicating a divine design—an intricate balance between the essential and the trivial, the impactful and the detrimental. It teaches us that a minority of causes yields a majority of results, a lesson that echoes through the ages.

The 80/20 Principle is a celestial brushstroke painting the canvas of our lives with balance and purpose. As we gaze upon its divine symmetry, we are reminded that harmony emerges when we acknowledge the vital few, strengthen their presence, and courageously eliminate the destructive many.

THE 80/20 FAMILY OPTIMIZER™

20% of Family Activity = 80% of Family Formation	20% of Family Activity = 80% of Family Destruction
"The 20%" The High-Impact Formation Activities	**"The 20%"** The High-Impact Destructive Activities
.	.
.	.
.	.
.	.
Action Items to Bolster the 20%	Action Items to Eliminate the 20%
.	.
.	.
.	.
.	.

CONCLUSION

Our decisions define us. We shouldn't take them lightly. But we can't cower in fear because of the magnitude of their impact on our lives. Discernment helps us understand this seriousness without allowing the moment to become paralyzing. The tools we've presented in this section are aimed at arming you with a foundational strength that only comes through the spiritual clarity of discernment.

Now you have resources to help focus your family, make decisions, and solve problems in a very intentional way. These tools are in no way a guarantee of 100 percent positive results and outcomes, but they should help you find a lot more peace in the process. They are a framework to help you and your family come to conclusions in a unified way. In my family, how we come to decide something often turns out to be much more important than the actual decision. This refined process of Discernment, combined with the five previous steps of Vision, Unity, Systems, Metrics, and Relationships completes The Well-Ordered Family Management System™.

CONCLUSION

This isn't the end for you. It is the beginning.

I envision your returning frequently to these pages as a reference book. I envision the pages highlighted and marked up, with sticky notes on your favorite tools for easy reference. The best way to treat this book is to beat it up. It is a tool and wants to be used.

If this book has served a purpose in your family life, it ought to be in helping you begin anew with a spirit of hope and joy.

I pray that whatever wisdom is contained in these pages will be taken by you, customized for your family, and made your own.

My family is different from yours. Yours is different from your neighbors'. Every family is unique. But, just as in business, there are fundamental guiding principles. These principles apply to every family, for they are based on universal human nature.

My goal as the creator of *Well-Ordered Family* is to provide you with a new beginning so that you can reclaim order and clarity in your family life.

Please, use this book and the resources available at *wellorderedfamily.com* to give your family the fresh start it deserves.

The best way for you to finish this book is to consider the family you love, think about all your hopes and dreams for them, and resolve to achieve this vision in God's good time. Then close the cover and say, simply, "Let's begin."